Here's the Situation

MIKE "THE SITUATION" SORRENTINO
and Chris Millis

A Guide to Creeping on Chicks,
Avoiding Grenades, and Getting in Your GTL
on the Jersey Shore

GOTHAM
BOOKS

GOTHAM BOOKS
Published by Penguin Group (USA) Inc.
375 Hudson Street, New York, New York 10014, U.S.A.
Penguin Group (Canada), 90 Eglinton Avenue East, Suite 700, Toronto, Ontario M4P 2Y3, Canada
(a division of Pearson Penguin Canada Inc.); Penguin Books Ltd, 80 Strand, London WC2R 0RL,
England; Penguin Ireland, 25 St Stephen's Green, Dublin 2, Ireland (a division of Penguin Books
Ltd); Penguin Group (Australia), 250 Camberwell Road, Camberwell, Victoria 3124, Australia
(a division of Pearson Australia Group Pty Ltd); Penguin Books India Pvt Ltd, 11 Community Centre,
Panchsheel Park, New Delhi—110 017, India; Penguin Group (NZ), 67 Apollo Drive, Rosedale,
North Shore 0632, New Zealand (a division of Pearson New Zealand Ltd); Penguin Books
(South Africa) (Pty) Ltd, 24 Sturdee Avenue, Rosebank, Johannesburg 2196, South Africa
Penguin Books Ltd, Registered Offices: 80 Strand, London WC2R 0RL, England

Published by Gotham Books, a member of Penguin Group (USA) Inc.

First printing, November 2010

1 3 5 7 9 10 8 6 4 2
Copyright © 2010 by Michael Sorrentino

LIBRARY OF CONGRESS CATALOGING-IN-PUBLICATION DATA
Sorrentino, Mike.
Here's the situation : a guide to creeping on chicks, avoiding
grenades, and getting in your GTL on the Jersey Shore /
Mike "The Situation" Sorrentino.
p. cm.
ISBN 978–1–592–40642–5 (pbk.)
1. Single men—Psychology. 2. Dating (Social customs)
3. Man-woman relationships. 4. Sorrentino, Mike. I. Title.
HQ800.3.S67 2010
306.81'520973—dc22
2010036290

Printed in the United States of America

Set in Cremona
Designed by Sabrina Bowers
Illustrations by Chris Millis

CONTENTS

PART III: AS PER LIFE

How small a fraction of all the measureless infinity of time is allotted to each one of us; an instant, and it vanishes into eternity. How puny, too, is your portion of all the world's substance; how insignificant your share of all the world's soul; on how minute a speck of the whole earth do you creep. As you ponder these things, make up your mind that nothing is of any import save to do what your own nature directs, and to bear what the world's Nature sends you.

—Marcus Aurelius, *Meditations*

Quoted from the Penguin Great Ideas Edition (2005), translated by Maxwell Staniforth

INTRODUCTION

Friends, bros, countrymen, lend me your ears. For The Situation has come to give you the situation.

In my twenty-eight years of crushing it, I have come to one simple realization: Life is a battle. It's you against the beat, fist against the air, skin against the sun, hair against gravity, bicep against dumbbell, wingman against grenade, and Escalade against summer Friday traffic to the Jersey Shore. Some will leave the field victorious with a hot chick on their arm, while others . . . well, do I really need to embarrass them further by writing about them here?

In this guidebook you'll find everything you need to win the battle of life. From creeping to blowouts to fist-pumps to GTL, The Sitch will give you the tools to succeed. You must only follow me to glory.

As Per the Use of the Word "Guido"

Ever since *Jersey Shore* blew up huge, politicians, pundits, and all kinds of other tool bags have been up in arms over the use of the word "guido." For the record, it's not a word I use with any frequency. But it really doesn't bother me unless it's intended in a derogatory way, as an insult against Italians and their heritage. People who get their Calvins all twisted into a bunch over that word need to realize that when it's used by me in a group of friends, it's as a joking sign of affection and camaraderie that goes back to the days of prehistoric kindergarten when we all thought the tooth fairy was alive. It's about celebrating a unique lifestyle. A lifestyle that embraces a certain look, an attitude, and the philosophy of GTL and crushing it 24/7.

When people get all pissed off about the word "guido" or our adventures that get aired on *Jersey Shore*, I have a simple suggestion for them: Don't watch the show. Nobody is forcing you to turn on MTV on Thursday nights at 10:00 p.m. (check local listings). Just like no one is forcing you to hit the gym and the tanning salon. Or forcing you to read this book. Or, for that matter, forcing you to have this book read to you by a naked chick like I'm doing right now.

The Sorrentino family has a rich Italian heritage. We keep a book at home that chronicles our story and I'm very proud of that history. The last thing I'd ever want to do is alienate any of my fellow Italian-Americans over a misunderstanding or simple semantics. So chill out, Freckles McGee.

And now let's start crushing it.

Here's the Situation

PART I:

As Per Pregaming:

GTL and Beyond

one

GYM

By now the entire nation knows of my holy trinity of gym, tanning, and laundry, aka GTL. Let's take this thing from the top, with *G*.

As a certified personal trainer, a former professional underpants model, and a guy who looks like Rambo, pretty much, with his shirt off, I know a thing or two about physical fitness. Now, I may be blessed with superior genetics (see next page), but I still hit the gym hard for ninety minutes, five or six days per week. If you want to develop a situation of your own, you can't be half-assed about your workouts. And if you're not locking down the G, you don't deserve to move on to the T and the L. Because it don't make no sense to tan a flabby midsection. Or to obtain crisp laundry to pull over withered biceps. It all begins in the gym. And that applies to everyone, not just world-famous individuals like The Situation. If you skip the gym, you're not going to perform at the peak of your abilities, whether it be at a job in an insurance office or starring on cable TV's highest-rated show in its most coveted demographic.

My fitness situation comes down to three things: Lifting, Cardio, and Nutrition. Like how God is simultaneously the Father, Son, and

Holy Ghost, the Situation *is* Lifting, Cardio, and Nutrition. These are indivisible and eternal.

GENETIC SITUATION

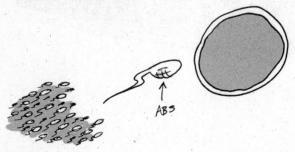

I've been blessed from the very beginning with genes that make me a winner.

Lifting

Big is out and lean is in. It's important to have a well-balanced physique, but chicks dig two things: biceps and abs. Moreover, these muscles will come in handy on a day-to-day basis. When you go to the dry cleaner to pick up your fresh shirts, what muscle are you going to use to pick them up? That's right: your biceps. And what happens if, on the way home from the dry cleaner, you spill some protein shake on your shirt? You'd need a washboard to clean them before the stain sets, right? Good thing you'd be carrying a washboard at all times in the form of your abs. Interplay like this is why GTL is a rock-solid system. I've thought this shit out, bro.

Here's the program I follow for huge guns and ripped-up abs that shock and awe:

Monday	Chest, Biceps, Abs
Tuesday	Back, Abs, Biceps
Wednesday	Biceps
Thursday	"Cheat Day" (read more on page 98)
Friday	Supersets of Biceps and Abs
Saturday	Abs (and possibly biceps)
Sunday	Biceps and/or Abs
Super Sunday	(This is an extra day that does not appear on traditional calendars. It only exists for individuals that have achieved an optimum level of fitness. On this day, I will typically work my biceps and abs.)

I like to incorporate situational training when working on my situation. I train my fist-pump muscles using a heavy dumbbell or a cable apparatus. (Pauly D and I are actually deep into R & D on a Fist-Pump 3000 Trainer.)

Coming to gyms everywhere in 2011

I'll also occasionally pick the biggest gorilla juicehead in the gym (although if he's in the gym with me, it's more accurate to call him the *second-biggest*) and invite him to pummel my midsection with punches in order to maintain my ab strength.

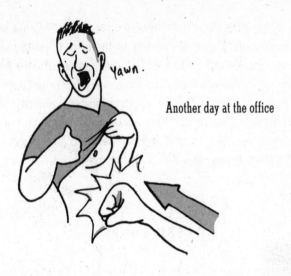

Another day at the office

SITCH AB FACT: My abs actually played the part of Vinny for the entire third episode of *Jersey Shore: Season One*. My abs are such good actors, no one noticed.

Cardio

If you want a ripped-up ab situation, you can't let that six-pack hide under a layer of fat. You've got to burn that off by hitting the treadmill for at least a half hour every day. Hours and hours on the treadmill might sound tough, but it's all part of being in the game. As with everything in life, you get out what you put in. For the best results, switch it up by also using the elliptical trainer and Stairmaster. You want to confuse your muscles by hitting them in different ways. Although my muscles are by this point nearly impossible to confuse; my abs are so intelligent they actually wrote this entire chapter.

You might ask yourself how a world-famous celebrity like me finds time to get in his cardio. Rest assured that while you're sitting on your couch watching reruns of *Jersey Shore*, in a hotel gym somewhere The Sitch is paying his bills on the treadmill.

Fresh Tunes

My preference is hard rock and hard rap when I'm pushing my body hard at the gym. That style of music gets me amped up and helps me sustain workouts for as long as I need (I suggest my debut single "The Situation" for your listening pleasure, though that may be too hard-core for beginners). And, yeah, sometimes I'll get so fired up listening to tunes that I'll throw a couple fist-pumps into my treadmill routine. That's called cross-training, bro.

Nutrition

If you want to look like The Situation, which is going to be pretty tough, you're going to have to get that protein in your diet. That means protein shakes and chicken cutlets all day every day. More than that, you have to eat clean. You can crush chicken Parm, but don't eat the spaghetti on the side. Pasta is awesome, but don't let carbs be the difference between a six-pack and a sick-pack.

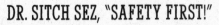

DR. SITCH SEZ, "SAFETY FIRST!"

Use caution! For your safety, I strongly recommend that individuals refrain from starting an intensive workout routine until they are least six to eight weeks of age. Of course, not everyone has the genetic benefit of superior muscularity and skeletal girth, so please, consult your pediatrician.

Proper Ab Maintenance (Step by Step):

Your abs are everything, dawg. And once you develop them, you gotta treat them right. Not taking care of your six-pack is like saving up for ten years to buy an Escalade, then not pimping it out with a set of dubs, a killer sound system, and a GTL 4 EVA vanity license plate. It just don't make no sense.

Step One: Crunch

Proper form will achieve maximum benefit. In the gym and the bedroom. Yo!

Step Two: Shave

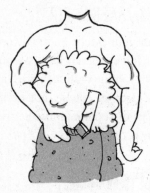

You can't cover that chiseled pack with fur, bro. Let your boys breathe.

Step Three: Tan (more on this in the next chapter)

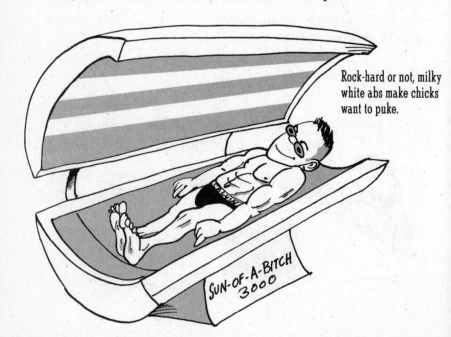

Rock-hard or not, milky white abs make chicks want to puke.

Step Four: Lubricate

Slicked-up abdominals encourage the ladies to slip and slide.

It's a little-known fact that I donate all my gym sweat. Several eco-forward companies are trying to develop it as a sustainable fuel source for green energy. In certain circles, it sells for a princely sum per ounce as a premium bronzer (all proceeds going to charity, of course). And in the Far East—I mean, even farther east than East Orange, New Jersey—it is revered as a powerful aphrodisiac when applied topically or ingested orally (the latter being not for the faint of heart). Read more about my charitable contributions in Chapter Eleven: Giving Back.

two

TANNING

What's the sense of molding your body into a rock-hard paragon of fitness if you're not going to get your skin did right? You'd have to be crazy to hit the beach with a pasty white complexion. To have no color is to not be alive. But the right tone—the one that brings out the color in your eyes and the definition in your abs—is different for everyone. Pauly D hits the tanning bed every day and has a deep golden hue that sets off his tattoos and dark features. But I've found that I look best when I get my color touched up twice a week. As a rule of thumb, think about the colors of the Italian flag. If you're red, you've tanned too much. If you're white, you haven't tanned enough. And if you're green, well, then you drank too many Jägerbombs the night before.

When it comes to tanning, you've got options:

A. The sun at the center of our solar system

B. Tanning beds

C. Spray tanning and bronzers

For generations humans have relied upon the sun to obtain that healthy glow. But the sun is an angry star—the angriest in our galaxy—and if not respected it can derail your game real quick. If you fall asleep on the beach at Seaside dreaming about creeping on chicks at Karma later that night, you'll wake up looking like a lobster. Then when you do hit the club you won't be creeping, you'll be crabbing. And that's just creepy.

Much more reliable than the sun is the tanning bed. I hit up the tanning salon right after I work out. It's part of my routine. I pop in the bed, set the timer, and relax. Strictly set it and forget it. When looking for a tanning salon, you want a place that's classy and upscale, with affordable pricing and staff packed with smoking-hot chicks. Note that many guys go freeballing in the bed, but I retain my Calvins. Because the last thing I want to deal with later on that night is a sunburnt sub-Sitch.

Now, if you somehow find yourself in an area with neither sun nor tanning beds (or if you're a pussy who's afraid of skin cancer), your only options are spray tanning and bronzers. These can do in a pinch, but don't rely too heavily on them. If you hit the spray tanning too hard, you're going to wind up looking orange and fake. And if fake is how you look, fake is how you'll feel. And that's no way to creep.

The Mix-and-Match

When you've reached a certain level of tanning acumen, you can combine natural sun, tanning beds, and bronzers into a triple-headed spear (aka a trident) of color. So I might hit up the tanning bed after the gym in the late afternoon, then top that off with an hour or two at the beach, and then before I creep the clubs later that night I might throw on a little bronzer.

The Tanning Tax and You

On July 1, 2010, the federal government began levying a 10 percent tax on all indoor tanning in order to pay for national health care. Now, I think it's great that everyone gets health care, but what's the point of living if you're not tan?

Looking over the numbers with my CPA Pauly D, I spent $1,828.94 on tanning in fiscal 2009. With the new tax, I'm looking at a nearly $200 hit per year. Is that going to keep me out of the tanning bed? That's like asking if overpriced drinks are going to keep me out of a club.

But I'm still looking to minimize my tax exposure. One thing I'm working on is having my political action committee, Sitizens for Situational Government, lobby Congress to expand the tax-advantaged Flexible Spending Account program to include tanning. The way I see it, it's the least I can do for my fellow Americans.

Proper Ab Display

Now that you've hit the gym hard and got just the right amount of color, your six-pack is in top form and it's time to show it off. There's no reason to keep those abs all to yourself. That's just selfish, bro. Share them with the world. On the next page is a chart that will give you a sense of the appropriate height to tug up your shirt for a variety of common occasions:

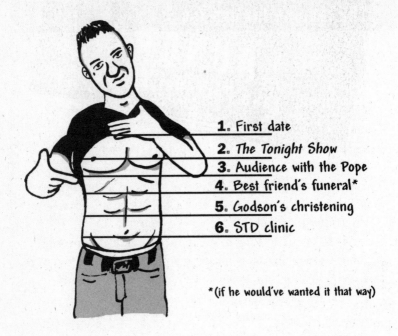

1. First date
2. *The Tonight Show*
3. Audience with the Pope
4. Best friend's funeral*
5. Godson's christening
6. STD clinic

*(if he would've wanted it that way)

SITCH AB FACT: Few know that I possess an extremely rare *seventh ab*—more rare than the albino elephant. So rare, in fact, that the show's producers worried its careless display might intimidate the audience, possibly causing spontaneous seizures. Therefore, each episode it must be hidden inside what has come to be known as "Snooki's poof."

three

LAUNDRY
(aka Personal Style)

The L in GTL is what's known as the Laundry Factor. But don't be confused. I'm not talking about simply washing and ironing your clothes or making routine trips to the dry cleaner's. (Although that's pretty freakin' important.) The Laundry Factor pertains primarily to how you assemble your outfits so that you look fresh for all occasions.

Once you've buffed out your body to maximum fitness in the gym, then brought out the shine in the tanning salon, you can't be draping baggy, faded clothes all over it. Wearing stylish, clean, and pressed attire is critical. When you look good, you feel good. And when you feel good, you creep good.

As Per Fitted T-shirts

Ninety percent of the time I roll into a club, I'm wearing a T-shirt. But we're not talking about a Hanes Beefy-T. We're talking about a silky-thin, fitted, designer number, ideally with metallic embellishments and embedded jewelry. It's like a knight putting on his armor, or a Delta Force commando pulling on his battle rattle.

For years the fine people at Ed Hardy, Affliction, and Christian Audigier have been outfitting me and my fellow hard-core creepers with sick T-shirts. But now you can take your shirt situation up to The Situation's situation with my own clothing line by Dilligaf. It's sick, bro.

Note that some cutting-edge shirts today include a necklace integrated into the garment itself. If you think this means you don't have to wear a separate, standalone necklace, you couldn't be more wrong.

Ask The Sitch

Purchasing the two halves of a track suit together, and in identical shades of the same color, is always recommended. But, for those rare occasions when the situation calls for a mix-and-match, here is a quick color-matching guide for pairing your up with your down:

Q: DOES NAVY BLUE GO WITH BLACK?
A: Never.

Q: CAN I ROCK A WHITE TOP WITH BLUE BOTTOMS?
A: Yes. But not the reverse.

Q: DOES VELOUR PAIR WITH NYLON?
A: Does a Fontodi Chianti Classico 2001 pair with a six-piece McNuggets? If you still don't know, the answer is no.

Q: TWO SHADES OF RED?
A: Depends. To be safe, be sure the darker shade is represented in the pants. And if by "shade of red" you mean pink, then the answer is no, no, no.

Q: HOW ABOUT KELLY GREEN AND . . .

A: Stop right there. Seriously, bro?

Fashion Fact. Most people make the assumption that I wear trendy shades the majority of the time (often indoors) to protect my eyes from the elements. But in fact it's the reverse. I'm protecting the elements from the brilliance of my eyes.

The Mathematics of Looking Fresh

People are always asking, "Sitch, how do you look so damn good in a deep-V T-shirt?" It's simple. I always apply the ancient geometric principle known as the Golden Ratio. Look, if you want to crush it like The Sitch, you can't phone it in, bro. You gotta do the work. When I'm rocking a deep-V, I'm always certain it will be unimpeachably pleasing to the eye of the beholder by first crunching the math on this time-tested formula:

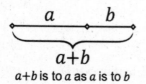

$a+b$ is to a as a is to b

Basically if you have two numbers, A and B, it has to be such that:

(A plus B) divided by A equals A divided by B.

So if your V-neck is 5 inches deep, make that A. The sleeve of your T-shirt must be 3.09 inches long, because 5 plus 3.09 is 8.09. Divided by 5 is 1.618. That's the left side of the equation.

And 5 divided by 3.09 is also 1.618. That's the right side of the equation. So they match. If your T-shirt meets these criteria when you roll into the club you will literally be a walking work of art.

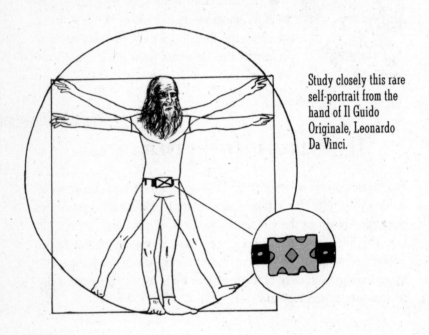

Study closely this rare self-portrait from the hand of Il Guido Originale, Leonardo Da Vinci.

Supplemental (RE: Belt Buckle Detail): Creepers will also benefit from this quick formula for determining the maximum allowable width of your belt buckle:

circumference of bicep — shoe size = Maximum Allowable Belt Buckle Width
(or MABBW, pronounced *Mabble-you*)

SITCH AB FACT: My abs are so cut that all my shirts have to be made out of Kevlar. Lesser fabrics are quickly shredded by coming into contact with my abs. (Sitch Fashion Tip: It's difficult to find military-grade Kevlar in Ed Hardy designs. But not impossible.)

Sitch Sez

No matter what T-shirt you select, whether it's fitted, graphic, sequined, bedazzled, crew-neck, deep-V, wifebeater, or what-have-you, it's about being proud of who you are. If you want to bust out a deep-V that's safety-cone orange because you think that's your color, then wear the hell out of that fruity shirt so everybody in the club knows that nobody owns it like you do. Set the trends, don't follow them. I wear what makes me feel good because I'm at the tip of the spear—the cutting edge of fashion that's fresh to death. When I see something I like, I grab it. My only system when I shop for fresh apparel is my own primal reaction to what I see, the moment I see it. When I enter a store, I trust my eye to zero in on what's mint. That's the single most effective system I have for knowing when to pull the trigger on a purchase. If I find myself hemming and hawing, that's a clear indication that the garment in question is not destined to make my rotation. I walk away from the rack because I've failed to make a connection to those threads. On the other hand, if I know from the moment I see it that that particular piece is going to make me look awesome, I trust my instinct completely and it comes home with The Sitch.

Shhhhh . . .
Here's an Exclusive Sitch Fashion Tip

If you're still having difficulty deciding whether or not to purchase a particular garment, there is one sure-fire method left at your disposal. Put the magnetic security tag gently to your ear. If you can hear the faint, distant thumping of bumping club music, buy it.

Real-Life Situation

In Spring 2010 I attended Mayor Michael Bloomberg's Inner Circle fund-raiser in New York City. As I slid on my brand-new outfit for the event, I realized that the staff at the clothing store had forgotten to remove the chunky plastic security tag from the front of my suit jacket. There was no time left before the limo arrived. I had no choice but to show up at the mayor's party wearing a jacket that looked like it was shoplifted on the way. Luckily, such minor issues leave The Situation unfazed. When I arrived, I simply removed my jacket and shirt, and wore nothing but a simple yet classy white necktie on my rippling bronzed torso.

On Tattoos

There was a time when every bro had a tribal armband tattoo over his biceps. But now the field of acceptable tattoos has grown to include the following categories:

Catholic (suitable iconography includes praying hands, rosary beads, and Jesus on the cross—bonus points if Jesus has ripped-up abs).

Brand logos (most commonly Ed Hardy and Cadillac, but also Red Bull and N.O.-Xplode workout supplement).

Familial (family name rendered in tasteful Italian flag motif, Nanna's chicken piccata recipe, etc.).

Personally, I've never gotten a tattoo because I put so much work into my physique that to cover it up with ink seems like a crime against nature. If someone is going to draw all over me, it's going to be in frosting, and she's going to lick it off afterward. But each bro should take his own counsel in this matter.

four

THE GTL REMIX

Now that we've got your GTL squared away, I've got a special treat for you, dawg. Are you ready to step your game up to the next level? Because I'm about to blow your mind.

What if you were to take your gym, your tanning, your laundry, and then top it off with a complete mastery of personal grooming? You'd have nothing less than the GTL Remix.

Hair and Eyebrows

As per my haircut, I always get it cut the day of an event, a photo shoot, a hot date, or wherever I need to be looking my freshest. Now, you might not be dressing up for the red carpet at the Grammys, but that doesn't mean you should be going out to the club with hair that's not tight. So do it right and get it cut day-of. And get your eyebrows threaded, too. When you're creeping on a chick, you want her gazing deeply into your haunting eyes, not checking out your bushy brows.

And don't be going to Supercuts. You want a barber whose *craft* is cutting hair. It's his art. He needs to wake up each morning thinking about cutting hair the same way I'm thinking about hitting the gym—with passion. That's why I get my hair cut once a week and my eyebrows threaded every two weeks at Justin's Barber Shop in Manalapan, New Jersey. Justin does me up right. If you're beyond an hour's commute from Manalapan (and why would you be, as that would mean you're precariously far from the Jersey Shore), I strongly recommend finding someone who can tighten up your fade like Justin.

Caesar Guido Augustus (circa 50 b.c.e.) is credited with history's first blowout. He had sick abs and was Rome's fiercest creeper. His personal maxim, creepito ergo smooshum, was later paraphrased by French philosopher René Descartes.

On Blowouts, Fauxhawks, et al

There was a time when every bro on the Jersey Shore wore the distinctive "blowout" cut, with every hair blow-dried skyward, then gelled and sprayed into a perfect flattop. Nowadays this style is something of a throwback, except for in Providence, RI, where it is still de rigueur. I prefer to rock a tight fade on the sides with a bit of style on top. Sometimes I'll even get lines or shooting stars shaved into the sides. You're welcome to try advanced styles like this, but be aware that your situation has to be functioning at a high level for you to pull it off. If not, I recommend sticking to the fauxhawk, which is a nice, safe style to roll with until you bring your situation up to the level of The Situation.

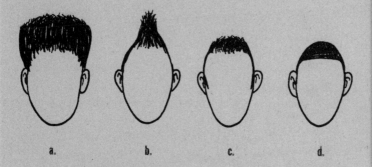

a.   b.   c.   d.

From left to right: a. Blowout. b. Fauxhawk. c. Tight fade. d. Tape-up

Scan these styles into your computer and drop in your photo to find the look that's right for you. Or, if you're still kicking it old-school, blow them up at Kinko's, cut a hole, and check yourself out in the mirror.

Shaving

I always wait until the last possible minute to shave so my face can be its smoothest for the longest possible time. If I'm hitting the club at 11:00 p.m. on a Friday, I'm not shaving Thursday. And I'm not shaving all day Friday, either. No blade is touching my face before 10:50 p.m. on Friday night. When that razor comes up, a fresh-faced Sitch is ready to get down.

As far as shaving the rest of your body parts, at a minimum you're going to want to shave your chest and six-pack. If you don't have a six-pack, you might as well stop reading here because I can't help you until you get your ab situation under control. I trim, but don't fully shave, my armpits. I don't make it a rule to shave my legs unless, as in the past, it's required for an underwear shoot and so forth.

Sitch Sez

While I don't recommend it as a permanent lifestyle choice, chicks do dig guys with shaved legs. Why? Maybe they're into the Michael Phelps look.

Fragrance

The final element of your personal grooming is your scent. Science informs us that men and women are attracted to each other through, among other factors, pheromones—i.e., the way we smell. It's critical that you consider the mood you're trying to convey and tailor your cologne accordingly. Whether that fragrance is Axe Body Spray Twist or Axe Body Spray Rise or Axe Body Spray Dark Temptation is all up to you.

My policy for selecting a scent goes right back to my policy for choosing clothing: I know in an instant whether I want it or not. It's the same with sexual attraction. A guy and a girl know in an instant whether or not they're destined to smoosh.

When it comes to picking a fragrance, things will get a lot easier for you in 2011. That's because the Situation cologne will be on the market. Pheromonally speaking, it's the one scent guaranteed to work in every situation.

On Nicknames

When your situation gets to a certain level, you're going to need a code name that encompasses who you are and what you bring to the table. Mine came to me naturally: I was walking along the boardwalk with some buddies (my abs exposed for the benefit of the masses) when a girl and her guy approached from the opposite direction. The girl literally stopped and stroked her hand across my abs—so mesmerized was she by my ripped torso, she couldn't restrain herself. My boys couldn't believe a chick would do that right in front of her man, so one of them said, "Whoa, that's a situation." I pointed to my abs and said, "No, *this* is The Situation." And so out of a real-life situation came The Situation.

Unfortunately for you, most of the best nicknames are already taken, such as The Situation, The Rock, The Unit (a friend of mine), Marky Mark (with or without the Funky Bunch), and The Solution, the moniker I bestowed on Conan O'Brien before he became "Coco"—which, not for nothing, isn't exactly the sort of handle that's going to have chicks throwing themselves at you. Ideally, your situation will be so strong that an awesome moniker will be bestowed upon you. If it doesn't happen spontaneously, here are some suggestions:

> The Foundation
> The Sensation
> The Inflammation
> The Conflagration
> The Haitian Nation
> His Emanation
> Zero Gravitation
> The Eradication
> Redonkulation
> Jason Space Station
> The Amalgamation
> The Abrasion
> The Emancipation Proclamation
> The Act of Persuasion
> The Asian Invasion
> My Caucasian Relation
> Autoerotic Asphyxiation
> Wartime Inflation
> Bill (short for William)

Real-Life Situation

I was in the terminal at LAX hustling to my cross-country flight back to JFK when I spotted this towering dude eyeballing me. He was a good distance away, but I could swear I recognized him. The guy was just about to board his flight, but stopped and put up his hand to tell the gate attendant to wait a minute. Then he pointed in my direction and started trotting over.

As he got closer, I realized I was looking at Dwayne Johnson—The Rock!

The Rock stuck out his massive hand to shake mine and said, "Situation, you're brilliant. America loves you. You've branded yourself and nobody even taught you how to do it!"

I'm a confident guy, but when I get feedback like that from a celebrity that I have immense respect for, I take it as the ultimate compliment and as serious validation. I hope to repay the favor by casting The Rock as my slightly less ripped partner in my upcoming big-budget action film *The Ab-breviators*. The tag line is: "They'll shorten anything. Including your life."

SITCH AB FACT: One of my rectus abdominis muscles, better known as my six-pack, has a holding deal with FOX for its own spin-off. Industry buzz is that it's a buddy-cop dramedy costarring Tom Green.

Some Final Thoughts

Gym. Tanning. Laundry. And now, the GTL Remix. When you put these key principles together and incorporate them into your daily life, I guarantee you're going to feel fantastic. And when you feel fantastic, you act fantastic. You exude confidence, no matter the situation. Adopting the GTL lifestyle says you take pride in your body and all the gifts God gave you. If you want your own situation, you will learn to live by this code.

PART II

As Per the Scene

five

THE JERSEY SHORE

Even if you're not familiar with MTV's breakout hit show of the same name, you likely already know that there's only one place on Earth that combines sun, sand, and DTF babes: the Jersey Shore.

Wintering

It's a long, cold winter in the Northeast. As warrior-poet Pauly D once said, "You can't tan in the winter. You can't creep in the winter. You can't do nothing in the winter." That's why you have to party hard all summer because before you know it, the days start getting shorter and the nights start getting colder. It's sad, bro. But that's why summer at the Jersey Shore is more intense than at any other beach in the world.

My abs wake from their involuntary slumber around late May.

But just because it's cold outside doesn't mean you should be hibernating. You can use the shirted months as a time to pack on muscle by lifting heavier and eating more chicken Parm. If you get a little heavier, that's okay. You'll have time to shed the fat before the sun returns from its winter siesta.* And make sure you're hitting up the tanning bed at least twice a month to keep your base coat primed. You don't want to be playing catch-up when Memorial Day rolls around. And of course, don't allow your dance muscles to

---

* Be grateful you're not The Sitch. Because there is no off-season when you're The Situation. I need to be able to show my abs year-round. It's a matter of national security.

atrophy—hit up those winter clubs (basically the junior varsity of clubs) every weekend to keep your moves fresh and your body limber.

(Keep in mind that, if your situation is at the right level, you just might find yourself spending the winter in beautiful Miami Beach with all expenses paid and the events recorded and broadcast on cable TV's highest-rated show.)

Getting There

As summer nears, you need to square arrangements for your share house down The Shore. Don't procrastinate on this critical element of your summer experience or you may find your GTL S.O.L. You can't creep without a headquarters, so establish your base of operations early with a solid group of trusted friends. The ideal share will have plenty of bedrooms, a grill, and of course a Jacuzzi.

That first Friday when you're preparing to leave work early and battle the traffic over the bridge, through the tunnel, and along the Garden State Parkway, you may find yourself so excited that you need to conference in all your bros on your cell and scream at the top of your lungs, "I'M GONNA POUND OUT EVERY BITCH FROM SANDY HOOK TO LONG BEACH ISLAND!"

This behavior is perfectly normal. And encouraged. You are experiencing the first stages of release from a long, miserable, dark winter. Your statement is only a metaphor for the fun you are about to have in the months ahead. But metaphor or not, it's still a good goal to strive for.

Vehicles

So how you going to get to the Jersey Shore? Don't tell me you're taking mass transit. That's for communists. You want to get yourself situated into a late model Escalade, or maybe a Range Rover, in either white or black. Because that's the only way to roll.

A luxury SUV is critical for weekend trips to The Shore, as it provides ample storage for T-shirts, protein supplements, and hair products. And it can fit up to ten guidettes when they're stacked on top of each other (including one Snooki-sized one in the glove box).

Ask The Sitch

Since I'm now chauffeured nearly everywhere in town cars and limos, I know some people are probably wondering if I ever pilot my own ride anymore. The answer is yes. I love to drive. In fact, when you get your own situation you'll definitely need to concern yourself with having a fleet of sweet rides in the garage for every situation. My brother and I share vehicles, which include a Range Rover, pickup truck, and Chrysler 300. In March 2010 I held an online auction for my hunter green, 1999 BMW 5-Series 528i, which I billed as the ultimate guido machine and a rare opportunity to own a piece of pop culture history. I also threw in a custom New Jersey GTL license plate that was given to me by MTV. Why did I auction my ride? Because it's my duty to give back.

As Per Your Environmental Situation

You might have noticed that I prefer vehicles that are as oversized as my personality, with a particular love for SUVs. Maybe these rides aren't the greenest ones out there. Alright, I admit it: A tricked-out Escalade gobbles fuel and spits out exhaust like Angelina chugs vodka and spews drama.

But I don't sweat it. Because what's the cleanest, most environmentally friendly source of power out there? Solar power, of course. And what am I, if not solar-powered? I absorb the sun's rays and convert them into fist-pumps. Soon, scientists will achieve the ability to harness the raw power of my fist-pumps. Just think, in a not-so-distant future, one night of me crushing it in the club could keep the Northeast lit for a year.

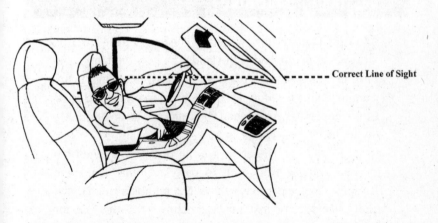

Correct Line of Sight

When he rolls in his ride, a dude should position himself as to minimally view the surrounding traffic through the opening in his steering wheel, approximately .0001 nanometers above the dash. That's plenty.

Can you guess these fresh vanity plates? (answers below):

1. NJCRPR
2. BANGME
3. SIKABS
4. FSTPMP
5. GFFPRZ
6. DWNSHR
7. GTLRMX

Answers: 1. New Jersey Creeper. 2. Self-explanatory. 3. Sick Abs. 4. Fist-pump. 5. Grenade-Free Foundation President. 6. Down The Shore. 7. GTL Remix.

Gassing Up Your Ride

You don't pump your own gas in The Jerz—it's the law. And it should be the law of the land. The very thought of citizens in other states—American citizens!—handling petroleum implements with their bare skin makes The Sitch sick. How can you stay fresh when you smell like an arsonist? Are we not men?

The traffic to The Shore can be brutal. You've got ten thousand people who want to party crammed onto one Turnpike. You've got to watch the exit numbers creep down from over 125 to that magical number 82—the exit for Tom's River and Seaside Heights. As you sit there, you're going to be tempted to cut it short, to hit exit 102 for Asbury Park or exit 98 for Belmar. My friends, don't do it. Stick with it and stay true till 82. As you exit the parkway and get onto route 37, your pulse should begin to rise. As you cross the mighty Barnegat Bay, you should pound an energy drink and bump your house music to the maximum tolerance of your SUV's speaker system. Soon enough you'll hear the seagulls and smell the salt air. At that point you'll know that it was all worth it, and that summer has officially begun.

Lost in the Pine Barrens

In the event you try an ill-conceived shortcut to avoid traffic to The Shore you run the risk of finding yourself hopelessly lost in the New Jersey Pine Barrens. Many a bro has found himself in this predicament, so I've constructed a survival guide to keep your game fresh until help arrives. A GTL Triage, if you will.

The Situation's Outdoor Survival Guide

Nutrition

The first thing you'll need to do is consume a protein shake to maintain your energy level. Construct a rainwater receptacle by turning an Ed Hardy tee inside out (to protect the graphic and various adornments) and stretching it between four vertical sticks. Weigh down the center with a tube of gel to channel fresh water into one of

those plastic cocktail cones that Snooki always drinks from. (Note: keep plenty of those cones handy. For Snooki and life-or-death emergencies.)

Use your iPhone to peel away pine bark, revealing the pulp and sap beneath (sorry, there's no app for this). Muddle together the water and pulp (mixing in sap and bits of pine bark to taste) until you have a thick protein beverage packed with dense nutrients. Set aside any excess sap for later use in case you run low on gel while skilling your backwoods blowout.

Gym

Most people attempting to rock their GTL in the great outdoors will try to fashion a dumbbell out of heavy stones, but that severely limits your isometric resistance. An experienced gym rat knows that live wood-land creatures are his best bet for hammering his biceps, Grizzly Adams style.

Being lost in the Pine Barrens doesn't exempt you from a minimum of thirty minutes of cardiovascular exercise per day. Rip a good-sized live tree from the earth with your bare hands and hurl it into the nearest body of water. Scramble your playlist and jump on to burn some serious calories so there's no flab hiding those abs.

Tanning

Whether you're working long hours behind a desk or fighting for your very survival in the unholy wild of the New Jersey wilderness, there's no excuse for letting your color fade. Your passenger-side mirror makes an ideal reflector to even out your tone under your chiseled jawline. As far as defacing your sweet ride, hey, if you want to make a protein-rich egg-white omelet, you've got to break a few organic eggs. Fortunately, New Jersey is a no-fault state, so when you get to The Shore, write down the number of the first license plate you see and report to your insurance carrier that their vehicle sideswiped you.

Laundry

In the wild, it's unlikely that your mom will be there to do your laundry. Possible, but unlikely. To get your L did right while flying solo, wade into the nearest stream and scrub your wifebeater back and forth along your anatomical washboard. When you see the spectacular results, you'll wonder why you haven't been washing your threads this way all along.

If you need to repair a loose sequin on one of your
fitted tees, have no fear. If you've gelled properly, you can remove a single hair from
your dome and fold it over to create an
emergency field needle. For thread, repur-
pose some from any garment you've worn
more than once in the past year. You'll be
back up and sparkle-fresh in no time.

GTL Remix

With some string and a pair of fashion denims, you can MacGyver
a respectable hair dryer from your Escalade's exhaust to get your
blowout done right. As mentioned above, if you squeeze out the last

drop of gel, hit the surplus pinesap for a hold that will stay firm through even the most hard-core partying.

SITCH AB FACT: In 2008, my six-pack became the first abdominals to perform an emergency appendectomy. On myself.

On Authenticity and The Shore

A lot has been made about the fact that I wasn't born in New Jersey. Blah-blah-friggin-blah. By now, most people realize that Sitch pays no mind to the haters. Their noise rolls right off my muscular deltoids like water off a duck phone's back. Like I always say, if hating is your occupation, I got a full-time job for you. Yes, I was born in Staten Island and moved to The Jerz as a kid. The way I see it, that's just more of a good thing, cementing my dual citizenship in two of the major guido capitals of the world. Salud!

The Jersey Shore is located at the heart of what's known as The Guido Belt. This is a region that stretches from Northern New Jersey (extending south along its coastline), through select boroughs of Metropolitan New York, to all of western Long Island. It

MAINE

VT

N.H.

NEW YORK

MASS.

CONN.

R.I.

PENNSYLVANIA

N.J.

MD

DEL.

W. VA.

VIRGINIA

also includes South Philly, parts of Baltimore, and Pauly D's Providence, Rhode Island.

A Glossary of Shore Speak

Battle: To beat up the beat.
Beat up the beat: To battle.
Busted: A grenade.
Creep: To crush it.
Crush (see also: Crushing it): To creep well.
Down The Shore: Heaven.
Fist-pump: The physical act of beating up the beat.
Fresh/fresh to death: Mint.
Grenade: A female human who is busted.
Mint: Looking fresh to death.
Vibe: The act preceding smooshing and/or pounding out.
Hippopotamus: A larger girl who is attached to her much more attractive friend.

Pregaming at the Share

Fellow warriors, your share house is your castle. That's where we prep for our battles at the club and that's where all our hot tubbing, pounding, and, for those special ladies, smooshing will happen after hours. Before hitting the scene, you're going to want to get in some pregame. Whether your drink of choice is Ron-Ron Juice or simple vodka tonics, you want to be well-lubricated by the time you leave the share. Think of pregaming as putting gas into a Ferrari before tearing off down the Parkway.

As you're getting your drink on, hit up some last-minute biceps curls so your guns are at maximum vascularity. Make sure your fade is tight and every hair on your head has been put into the perfect position and held there forevermore with Ice Spiker. And, of course, save the shaving for last. Your share house should have copious mirrors so that you can secure views of yourself from all conceivable angles. You need be sure you look mint and feel fresh to death for what glorious adventures await.

A rookie mistake when pregaming is to wear your club shirt while doing so. While you're sitting on the couch, you're putting creases in your freshly pressed tee, and you're running the risk of spilling a beverage on yourself. That's not fresh. So veterans know that there's The Shirt, and there's The Shirt Before the Shirt. This is a wifebeater you wear while pregaming. When it's time to hit the club, you put your fresh to death T-shirt on over your wifebeater, and then you roll. Simple as that, dawg.

Sit-ups required to burn off these popular boardwalk staples:

Saltwater Taffy	25
Kohr's Frozen Custard	50
Funnel Cake	100
Deep-Fried Oreo	125
Oversized Boardwalk Slice	200
Jell-O Shot Taken from Between Girl's Breasts	225

six

CREEPING IN DA CLUB AND ELSEWHERES

So why is it so important to get in your GTL? Because GTL puts you in your best possible position to creep. And what is creeping? It's presenting yourself to females in such a way that smooshing follows soon thereafter. Simply put, to live is to creep. And vice versa.

Now, chicks may object that bros simply look at them as creeping targets. But chicks like being crept on. Sure, they'll tell you that they go to clubs simply to dance and have fun with friends. But take it from The Sitch, single people are at the club for one reason and one reason only: to not be single anymore. Even if it's just for that night.

So I creep.

The primary environment for creeping is a club—preferably down the Jersey Shore. Below are all the secrets you need for a successful night. The key is to not rush it. You need to pick a strategic spot in the club, display moves on the dance floor, and imbibe heavily. Then and only then are you ready to crush it.

Spotting a Fake Guido

Since the fist-pump and blowout first exploded into the pop-ular culture, plenty of poseurs have started hitting the club with their phony guido game. I'm talking about the orange bottle-tan, the rub-on tats, the fake gold, and the fugazi threads. My motto is "to each his own," but as a courtesy to The Sitch, keep that garbage outta my face. You can't be a little bit pregnant and you can't fake the GTL lifestyle. It's go hard or go home, bro. (And by the way, if you know anyone who's a little bit pregnant, it wasn't me.)

Positioning

Once through the door, scan for chicks who are clearly checking out your group and vibing on your collective style. That's where you'll be best served when focusing your initial efforts. But be careful when scanning *only* for hotness. Do this at your own peril. You may be severely limiting your selection in the long run. You want to look not just for hot girls but also for a large number of girls relative to the amount of gorilla juiceheads. I love sausage, but only when served with a side of my mom's peppers and onions. A sausage fest in a club is a no-go.

I typically like to set up a base of operations in the corner of a club—optimally with a table to hold me and my team members' Red Bull and vodkas—so that I can get the lay of the land. In my crew, I'm both Team Leader and in charge of advanced reconnaissance. I usually walk a few laps around the club on scouting missions, check-ing out the available females, and lay the groundwork for developing situations. Then, in conference with my team, we decide whether we're headed east, west, or straight up the gut. When the attack plan is set, we launch a calculated assault on the club zone where the hot chick–to-dude ratio is clearly in our favor.

We shall creep in the gym and at the tanning salon. We shall creep with growing confidence and a growing vibe. We shall avoid grenades, whatever the cost may be. We shall creep on the beaches and the boardwalk. We shall creep in da club, at the bar, on the dance floor, and in the general area of the DJ. We shall never surrender.

—Winston Churchill, Nobel Laureate/Statesman/Historian/Creeper

Beverages

Personally, my favorite drink in the club is anything given to me free, because I'm famous. For those who must purchase their own, here's what I recommend:

Top Five Club Drinks

1. Vodka and ice
2. Vodka and Red Bull
3. Vodka and Vitaminwater
4. Vodka Smoothie
5. Devotion Vodka (which is the only vodka to include protein and is endorsed by yours truly. I got your back, bro.)

Proper Stance

In da club, you need to consider your profile while hefting your beverage to maximize biceps bulge. To show off those guns you've been forging all week in the gym, here are three of the most effective arm curls seen down The Shore, made popular by the cocktails that inspired them:

1. The Heinie Grab

2. The Goose Neck Choke

3. The Bull by the Horns (note: Red Bull cocktails only)

Beating Up the Beat

At some point you're going to want to hit that dance floor, because there's no way you can stand the beat pumping through your body without surrendering to its gravitational pull.

Fist-pumping became a club necessity when the dance floor got so crowded from the bumping house music that the only place left to dance was up. To execute the perfect fist-pump, follow these simple steps: Listen to the music, feel the beat, and let your body begin to respond unconsciously. Go only with what feels right in that moment. Don't worry about what looks polished. Who cares what some gorilla thinks while he's watching you vibe on the floor? Why is some dude looking at you, anyway? Close your eyes and start furiously pumping your fist at the air. That's right, not into the air, but *at* it. You've got to beat back that beat. Battle it, bro. You can't let it win. The deep, thumping bass seizes hold of your every corpuscle. Let the beat strip away those last vestiges of self-conscious embarrassment as you pound, pound, pound the air into rhythmic submission. Battle harder. Keep battling, dawg. Never surrender.

Ah, but in the end, the beat always wins. As it always should.

The Overhead (aka classic pump)   The Flatliner   The Downward Pump (great for showing off the triceps)

Memorializing the Occasion

When you're looking fresh to death in the club, you're going to want to take some digital pictures to preserve the night for all of eternity. What else are you going to post on Facebook the next day? But it's critical you get your look right. If you're a dude, you can either go with a hard-core stare into the camera, or an air-kiss. There is no third option. Chicks have to roll with the duck-face or the trout pout, as it sometimes makes guidettes temporarily appear ten times hotter. (Aside to dudes: Don't be fooled by these nefarious pictures posted on Facebook.)

Doesn't matter how hard they mug for the camera.
These guidettes are still fugly.

Blood on the Dance Floor

You take a couple hundred juiceheads, give them tons of alcohol and energy drinks, and set them loose in a club with hundreds of chicks who are DTF. What's going to happen? Fist-pumping, smooshing, and definitely some fighting. And because of the high quality of work you do, you might be the target of a bro who's jealous of the chicks you're nabbing.

Resist the urge to be macho about it. You don't want to throw down, because you can't creep with a black eye and blood on your previously fresh-to-death T-shirt. But when you see two gorillas squaring off, keep an eye open for any females who might become single as their boyfriend gets mauled in a fight. A creeper creeps. And the creep never sleeps.

For a conflict-free night of creeping, avoid confrontation with this volatile—and extremely unpredictable—primate.

As Per the Fog of War

When you're in the club and you're ten drinks deep, the fog of war might descend upon you and you might have trouble communicating with your team. That's why Pauly D and I developed our elaborate (and trademarked) low-five routine. In the heat of the club, with thumping bass making verbal communication impossible, Pauly D and I can exchange a series of low-fives that gets across everything necessary. For instance, three low-fives means, "Let's go creep on some chicks," whereas two low-fives followed by a chest bump means, "Let's go get some more drinks, and then let's creep on some chicks." Being able to convey subtle messages such as these in the midst of battle is crucial to team success.

Approaching Your Target

When you've had your share of beating up the beat and can feel the twelve energy drinks you've consumed coursing through veins, your heart pumping in rhythm with the fresh house music thumping from the speakers, you're finally ready to engage Situation Mode. By this point in the night, you've probably noticed a few females vibing you. Now, it's time to approach. So many bros get all hung up on pickup lines, as if it really matters what you say to a girl. If you've chosen your target correctly, the first thing you say to her is merely a formality. I don't even have to think about it anymore, as I have the world's best opening line: "Hi, I'm The Situation."

I'm not one for using pickup lines to meet chicks. Honestly, I have so many chicks rolling up to me these days that I have to come up with lines to get them to leave me alone. But take heart. All any girl is looking for in a guy is that he's positive, charming, charismatic, confident, honest, rich, world famous, and has thunder abs.

Glow Sticks

Some prefer to battle the beat with their own source of illumination: fresh glow sticks. This has never been part of The Situation's situation, but I understand the appeal. As the neon glow cuts through the gloom of the club, all females get to see your sick moves (in the general area of your neck and shoulders anyway). However, don't appear too polished with your glow stick moves, as chicks will surely infer that you spend too much time practicing your routine in front of the mirror.

SEAL the Deal

Because life is a battle, and those battle lines are never more clearly drawn than in da club, I'm fond of comparing the tactics of my boys and me to the precision fierceness of our badass U.S. Navy SEAL teams. Though my team also rolls in with military discipline, it's nothing compared to the exacting ferocity of our brother creepers in special ops. In the spirit of their can-do attitudes, and on-the-fly decision-making skills, the term "SEAL" has evolved in clubcraft parlance into "Situation's Evolving Ad Lib." This acronym is code for when you and your wingman need to run a game, off the cuff, in a head-to-head firefight with two chicks. Like our warrior brothers in the armed services, you must be conversationally limber; able to react and navigate the twists and turns of verbal jujitsu that will impede your progress if you remain determined to close the deal and achieve your objective. A typical SEAL conversation might run like this:

SITCH: Yo, shake it baby. Drop it like it's hot.

HOT CHICK: What's up?

SITCH: You look fine tonight.

GRENADE (STUMBLES OVER): I'm tired, Angela. Let's go.

WINGMAN (TO GRENADE): Nah, girl. Let's get you another one of those Jell-O shots.

GRENADE: Only if you make it two. And maybe get one for yourself while you're at it.

WINGMAN: (Sigh).

SITCH (WHISPERING): Want to come back to my crib? I got a hot tub.

GRENADE: That sounds fun.

SITCH (TO GRENADE): Anyway, this hot tub is very small. It can't really accommodate more than two people.

GRENADE: I think I'm gonna be sick.

WINGMAN: Try this Jägerbomb. It'll counteract the Jell-O shots.

GRENADE: I think I, like, love you or something. (She slaps him.) I hate you.

WINGMAN (TO SITCH, ANNOYED): Clock's ticking, bro.

GRENADE (TO WINGMAN): Don't cond-send me. I'm smart. Hey,

Angela, you have a boyfriend! (Slaps wingman.) I totally love you.

SITCH: So whaddya say? You coming home with me or what?

ANGELA: I don't even know you.

SITCH (LIFTS SHIRT): What more do you need to know?

GRENADE (VOMITS): I need my stomach pumped.

WINGMAN: Yo! I need my fist pumped.

(WINGMAN AND SITCH HIGH FIVE.)

GRENADE: Where's the hospital?

ANGELA (FONDLING SITCH'S SIX-PACK, TO GRENADE): I'll call you a cab.

Once you've made contact, you have to identify who's a grenade and who's DTF.

What Is DTF?

When Sitch is on the road, I love to creep the local talent. A fun trip away from home can be made all the more enjoyable when I am pleasantly surprised by the sheer volume and variety of beautiful women in a given locale. Never have I been more delighted by this than when I first visited the Midwest. Throughout my appearances in Ohio, Michigan, and Minnesota I was blown away by the beauty and charm of the women I met. I remember entering a sold-out appearance at a club in Detroit where the ratio of beautiful girls to guys was at least 7 to 1. Certain cities have an energy all their own and that Detroit event was definitely unique. So many girls were screaming their lungs out and hysterical crying—it was absolutely insane! When I entered, all the women in the club were chanting, "DTF! DTF!" as a take-off on GTL. I had no idea what they were referring to and neither did the rest of my team. The club owner sensed my confusion so he yelled in my ear over the mayhem, "It stands for Down To Fuck." I confirmed later that night that these chicks were as serious about DTF as I am about GTL.

Beyond the Club

You don't have to limit your creeping to the club. When your situation is working at a high level, you can creep just about anywhere: at the gym, at the tanning salon, while picking up your laundry, during the ride from the gym to the tanning salon, etc. The whole world gets creepy when you're doing it right.

seven

WINGMEN AND GRENADES

The club, my friends, is a battlefield. And you should treat it as such. You need to roll in there like a special ops platoon on a mission. Your target: banging a chick. Anything that gets in the way of that mission should be dealt with swiftly and with no mercy. But it's never that easy. Because like in any war zone, you can get killed in the club. And death will usually come via grenade.

Grenades

It's a rule of the universe that, more often than not, there is going to be a good-looking girl and then there's going to be the grenade. A grenade is defined as the least attractive of the pair, or group, of females you are trying to close the deal with. Invariably, the grenade will spend the night complaining, with her arms crossed, and will usually at some point try to leave the club, taking her hot friend with her and out of your target range. Grenades are not to be underestimated, because they can go off at any time, and the collateral damage can take out you and your whole team.

Typical grenade.

Nine out of ten times, the grenade is a grenade because she's ugly and fat. She's mad at you and at life because everyone is more interested in her hot friend. (On rare occasions, a cute girl can slide into grenade status because of a horribly bitchy personality, or for being obsessive and possessive about the guy she wants to be with. But possessive chicks are better described as Stage Five Clingers, which we'll get to in Chapter Eight.)

Scientific researchers at The Creeper Institute for Situationomics have recently charted the most accurate neural map ever constructed of the mind of a grenade. In the spirit of my ongoing commitment to offer all pertinent information leading to the optimum hookup, I now make that map available for the first time:

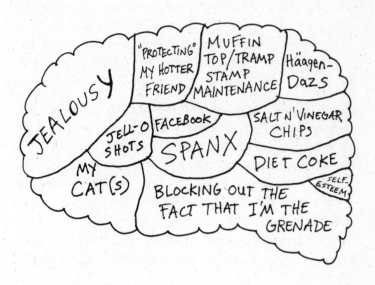

So what do you do when a grenade rolls in and threatens to detonate in the middle of your situation? Just like when a grenade rolls into a foxhole, a brave team member must pounce on it, absorbing the blast and protecting the lives of his team members. That brave soul is your wingman.

Explosive Situations

There are three different levels of grenades you'll encounter on the battlefield, so here's what to watch out for:

Standard-Issue Ordnance: Your run-of-the-mill grenade. She will roll up to your team accompanying a hot chick, and your wingman doesn't have much time to smother her before she inflicts serious casualties. Thankfully, she can be easily neutralized by a seasoned wingman. Most grenades are fat, but skinny ones do exist. We call these "land mines" because they can catch you by surprise.

The Grenade Launcher, aka the Rocket-Propelled Grenade, aka the RPG: This one is a bit trickier, as a Grenade Launcher has much more range than your Standard-Issue Ordnance, and thus can cause a lot more damage—even after you think you've gotten away from her or before you realize you're in her sights. Wingmen must take a proactive stance with RPGs, working to quickly redirect the blast away from the team. In this case, you must fight fire with fire. This volatile ordnance is best neutralized with a counteroffensive of Jägerbombs.

The Improvised Explosive Device, aka the IED: This is the gravest threat you'll encounter in the club. Like our brave troops serving overseas, you can never be sure when you'll encounter an IED. And once you find that you have one in your midst, you often won't have time to escape the blast radius. That's why you have to defuse an IED. I make my team watch the film *The Hurt Locker* every night before we head out into battle, to remind them of the seriousness of IEDs. Only the most experienced wingmen should attempt to tackle an IED.

Your Bro Above All Other Bros: Your Wingman

Your wingman is the most important member of your team. He can steer females your way and, most importantly, take out the grenades you will inevitably encounter. Your games should be complementary, enabling you to handle whatever females wander within your coordinates.

Of course, wingman status is a very fluid thing, and there will come times where you yourself, for the survival of the team, may find yourself taking out a grenade.

Real-Life Situation

This happened to me recently when there was an attractive female who I was interested in but she was more attracted to my buddy. Her friend liked me, but she wasn't as attractive as the girl I had my eye on. Don't get me wrong, she was a pretty girl—certainly not a full-on grenade— but at the same time I was a little disappointed that her hotter friend was pursuing my buddy instead of me. Listen, your relationship with your wingman is a constant give and take. You're going to have your nights when you're the victor with all the spoils and then you're going to have your nights where you've got to slog through the muck. All I can say to myself when that happens is, "Oh, well." Then I dig in, down my Red Bull and vodka, and carry on with the party. Hey, if creeping was easy, everybody would be doing it.

It's a common misconception that your wingman must be less attractive than yourself. Not true. The ideal wingman is a friend who is good-looking and has style, game, and a swagger all his own. Your ideal wingman can hold the line when it comes to meeting and leaving the club with women. You want a wingman who's a good-looking guy who will attract beautiful women because it increases the odds of you *both* hooking up with hot chicks. It's a game of strategy and numbers with glorious highs and spectacular lows. But that's the beauty of it. You just never know how the evening will play out. Your wingman must pull his own weight both mentally and physically. The perfect wingman is flexible and open to shifting circumstances.

Shhhh: The Secret About Grenades

Another misconception is that the better sex is always to be had with the hotter chick, but it can be argued that indeed the best sex is often with the grenade—because she's so grateful. Some grenades are known to lose their minds in the sack because they never know when they will be back there again with a willing partner. In these cases, it's your lucky wingman that will be thanking you over breakfast. Fact is, I know guys who prefer the grenades because it's less of a challenge. They're grenade-pouncers and proud of it.

The worst kind of grenade is a grenade who doesn't know she's a grenade. They remind me of those early contestants during the audition stage on *American Idol.* It's just sad, bro.

Not all wingmen are perfect, and you must constantly evaluate if you've chosen the right partner. The first sign of a subpar wingman is when you're paired off with a couple chicks and your buddy can't hold his own with his lady, resulting in her ruining your time with the chick you're trying to get with. If your wingman is not able to stabilize the situation with his girl, then he's no wingman. The ideal wingman must possess the requisite charm and charisma to supplement your excursions into the female wilderness, or you need to cut the cord, because he ain't your boy.

Real-Life Situation

There are times when even the best wingman fails to come through. On a recent trip to Houston, I had convinced a couple girls to accompany me and my wingman back to the hotel. These girls were down from the jump. My wingman told me to go ahead to my room, settle in, and he'd send the girl I was hanging with straight up. This struck me as a sound plan until I found myself lying on my bed, watching cartoons, and waiting far too long for the girl to arrive. I texted my wingman, "Hey bro . . . Where's the girl?"

No response.

This was highly unorthodox. I began to suspect that something odd was afoot. I texted again: "Yo? Wingman? What happened? Where's the girl that was headed to my room?!"

About fifteen minutes later, I got a text back: "She's on her way."

When she arrived she said that, after her friend had bailed on her, she went ahead to my room—but accidentally arrived at my wingman's door first. She decided that he was pretty cute, too, so she made a pit stop before continuing on to the main event. This may have worked out splendidly for my wingman, but I view this as a complete breakdown in protocol and The Wingman Code. His mission was to send her on to my room, not invite her into his own. He broke the cardinal rule by steering his gear into the path of my chick. But I forgave him. In that instance it was really more a case of where, when you're rolling with a confident, good-looking crew, some chicks are just down for the whole team. And besides, a great wingman is hard to replace.

Ask The Sitch

Q: WHAT'S THE SITUATION'S TAKE ON SLOPPY SECONDS?

A: That depends on many factors. For instance: How late at night is it? Is there an opportunity to establish untainted relations with a different female (always preferred)? This is an instance where a guy must do the math and rationalize the best approach to a girl who may have just had sex with your friend ten minutes prior. If you decide to pursue, be sure to avoid all bodily crevices where your friend's fluids may have accumulated.

Real-Life Situation

Troopers know how to play the wingman, even when they find themselves in an unfamiliar platoon. Not too long ago I found myself leaving a club in Vegas with fifteen girls in tow. Just me and fifteen girls! I don't know what the fuck I was thinking. A hotel security guard escorted me up to my room and the dude was looking at me like I was the grand marshal of the Thanksgiving Day Parade. More accurately described, it was like The Situation's Drill Team, with me being the drill.

But I realized I had a problem. There's a lot of Situation to go around, but fifteen chicks!? Even The Situation's bed has a maximum occupancy. We were all in the same elevator together and traveled up a few floors before the elevator stopped and opened for some guy who was waiting. The guy looked at me, the security dude, and the fifteen girls and said, "Situation, I love you, man."

Thinking on my feet, I said, "Bro, what's up? Get in here. There's plenty of room."

I played like I knew the guy, like he was a friend of mine, and he, a natural wingman, went right along with it. When we got up to my suite, he took one of the chicks with him into a spare bedroom, thereby reducing an unmanageable fifteen girls to fourteen, which I was able to handle on my own. That's a clutch wingman, and probably the luckiest dude to ever wait for an elevator in a Vegas hotel. (Read more about my tricks for handling multiple partners on page 83.)

My favorite pastime is proving people wrong about me. My second favorite pastime is pounding out a tight Seaside guidette. I also enjoy funnel cakes.

Sitch Sez

Closing the Deal

When your wingman has been deployed onto a grenade, the clock is ticking. It's only fair that, while given the opportunity to work your best moves while your wingman scrambles to diffuse the grenade, you must close the deal with all due haste. You're leaving your boy in harm's way, so if you can't make it happen with the hotter of the two chicks in a given time frame, you have no one to blame but yourself when the grenade explodes in both your faces. If you can't accomplish the objective in a reasonable length of time, your wingman has every right to abort the mission, jettison his canopy, and hammer his eject button. From that point on, it's every man for himself.

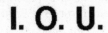

I. O. U.

ONE GRENADE

When presenting this coupon, the bearer promises, at a future date, to dive upon his wingman's grenade, no questions asked, no matter how heinous-looking or annoying that bitch is. No matter how much she talks about her cat(s) or who will, or will not, friend her on Facebook. This is the Wingman's Code.

Clip and store in your wallet, or between your fat roll of cash, wrapped twice with a rubber band.

Your Karma Situation

Karma is a bumping club in Seaside Heights, but did you know it's also an ancient Eastern philosophy? Basically it states that you receive back from the universe the same energy you send out into it. So, if I find myself diving on my third grenade in as many nights, that's a clear indication that my buddy is on a roll and I need to step up my game to the next level. My buddy isn't the problem, I am. It's not his fault I'm being fed all the grenades. That's an indictment of my skills and not anything I'm entitled to blame on him. He's out there doing good work (for himself, and for humanity). If I want to hook up with hotter chicks, no one's going to lead me by the hand and help me do it. We may enter the club as a team, but in the end, it's every man for himself when it comes to pounding and smooshing.

When you have found your perfect wingman, someone who abides by The Wingman Code and the GTL lifestyle, proudly present him with this:

—— OFFICIAL WINGMAN BADGE* ——

SITUATION-ISSUE

*Cut out and have your regular jeweler coat in platinum. (In the event of a down economy, 24-karat gold can suffice.)

Real-Life Situation: The Pre-Creep Hookup

Or, you can avoid the club altogether. At a spring break event in Panama City, Florida, I arrived at the hotel straight from the airport at about midnight. The streets were mobbed with college kids. I got settled in my room, then decided to take the elevator downstairs with a buddy so we could stand out front for a smoke. I was outside the front entrance for literally two minutes of quiet relaxation and warm ocean breezes when a large group of college students spotted me from a distance and ran toward me in a full sprint, screaming my name. I visited with them for a bit, then my buddy and I went back into the hotel. In the elevator, as the doors were closing, two chicks from the group jumped inside at the last possible moment. Long story short, I stepped outside for a smoke and the next thing I know I'm back in my room for the night with two hot college chicks. And they say tobacco is bad for you.

SITCH AB FACT: One of my abs is a classically trained pianist. Can you guess which one?

eight

STICKY SITUATIONS

When you bring your situation up to the level of The Situation, you just might find yourself in some sticky situations, whether it's a chick you've just smooshed or some hater who's jealous of the work you do. That's why you gotta have exit strategies.

One-Night Stands

When you bring a chick from the club back to your share house, things should progress quickly from there. It's the Jacuzzi, and then up to your private quarters for some pounding out. After you've done your work, you need your rest. But then what happens if the chick won't bounce? Or what happens if you're at her place and she has her claws dug into you?

Some chicks get all amped up after getting down with The Sitch—which is perfectly understandable. To ease her into La La Land, you may need to whisper a bedtime story into her ear to hasten the sandman and lay some lead on those lids. Here is one of my favorites:

Grenade-i-Locks and the Six Abs

Once as per a time in the forests of New Jersey there lived a Pappa Ab, a Mamma Ab, a Baby Ab, and three other abs. After crushing it all night in the club, they woke the next morning and blended their wake-up protein shakes, setting them in the refrigerator to cool. Then the six abs piled into their Escalade and rolled into the village to hit the gym, get some color, and pick up their dry cleaning. Soon after they left, a sloppy-drunk chick named Grenade-i-Locks, with strawberry Jell-O shot stains soaked down the front of her fugazi Prada blouse, stumbled into their crib. Grenade-i-Locks was basically a zoo creature who smelled food at the house. She was starving (she was always starving), and when she saw the feast the six abs were coordinating she began to scarf down all their shakes, nutritional supplements, and even threw their marinating chicken cutlets and surf and turf onto the grill. Then she fell asleep or whatever. The six abs came home and said, "Yo! This psycho bitch ate all our shit! Is she mindgaming us?!" So the six abs dragged Grenade-i-Locks outside by her extensions and stomped her ass until one of her fake tits popped out. Suddenly, they heard the wail of approaching sirens. And since most of the abs were on probation, they fled into the wilderness. The end.

Hopefully, at story's end, your one-night stand will be in deep REM, snoring like a buzzsaw. But, if the chick still won't go to sleep, here are some proven strategies that The Sitch has used to jettison a lingerer:

The "Early Departure"

This strategy requires the use of your wingman. (Note: If you're famous, you may also consider using your road manager or another member of your entourage.) Have him call your cell—or better, knock on your door—and remind you that you have an early flight. This works best when your buddy can physically lurk in the doorway until the chick gathers her things and leaves with him. If you employ this tactic while staying in your share house down The Shore, watch out you don't run into her the next night at Karma. That is not going to go well.

The "Bro in Need"

When she's not looking, text a buddy to call your cell. Then, run this script:

> (Phone rings.) "Yo. Whoa, buddy, calm down. What's the trouble? Where are you? Okay, sit tight. I'm on my way."

(End call.) "I'm sorry, baby, I gotta go. My best friend needs my help. I'll wait while you get dressed."

The "Social Network"

If you don't care if you ever see a girl again, and you don't want her number, you can be very direct while still remaining polite. There's no benefit to being a jerk to a girl, regardless of the circumstances, so when you really want to give her the brush-off, the line is: "Listen, sweetheart. I had a great time. I'll Facebook you." She'll know then that you're basically saying, "See you later, babe. But not really."

The "Li'l Sis"

Tell the girl that your little sister just got dumped by her boyfriend. She's hysterical and you need to go comfort her. Not only will this score you a fast exit (you are literally allowed to run from the building), but it will endear you in the eyes of the chick you're blowing off. This could lead to her telling her friends what a sweet guy you are, and down the road, you might be able to pound out one of them, too.

The "Point Blank"

You also need to be prepared for the chick who, no matter what tactic you try, simply won't leave. That's not a fun situation. Your only play is to be very forward with her: "Listen, sweetheart, I had a lot of fun tonight. This wasn't a joke. Leave me your number and I promise I'll give you a ring tomorrow. But I've got to get some sleep and I need you to go home. Now." She will find your honesty refreshing.

SITCH AB FACT: To fall asleep, my abs count abs jumping over abs.

Handling the "L-Bomb"

When your situation is tight and girls are flocking to you, you're going to run into situations when a chick drops the L-bomb on you. So what do you say when a girl tells you she loves you? You say, "Awesome." And that's it. What do you do if she again tells you that she loves you? You roll.

Any conversation that begins with a chick telling you she loves you is bad news, my bros. She's going to take whatever you say to mean that you care for her, too, even if you never send an L-word sailing back at her on a wave of soft kisses. The Sitch himself has made this mistake. It only prolongs the pain and kills your game. An impromptu L-bomb is how a cool hookup can morph into a clinger right quick.

Multiple Partners

If you follow all my advice in this book and start creeping like a pro, you'll soon find yourself faced with going home with chicks in precariously unmanageable numbers. Part of the reason I find myself in these type situations is because I'm so polite. I just can't bear to say no to anyone who wants to party with The Sitch. Plus, I don't discriminate. Some days I like vanilla ice cream, some days I like chocolate, and some days I go for cookies 'n' cream. Deciding on just the right flavor can be the most difficult part of my day—or, I should say, night. That's why I like to invite everyone back to my crib in an effort to delay my last-minute decision, depending on my appetite.

Real-Life Situation

One night in Detroit, I brought nine girls back to my hotel room. I don't know what I was thinking. It was pretty crowded, and I was exhausted, so I offered them an ultimatum designed to clear the room. I said, "Listen girls, I have another city to go to tomorrow. I don't want to be like this, but if you're not DTF (as previously advertised back at the club), then please exit the room immediately in an orderly fashion." I used a joking tone, but I was serious. I was tired and had an early flight.

All nine chicks exchanged glances, then smiles. No one made for the door. They were all enthusiastically DTF.

I said, "You gotta be kidding me."

I suppose, in theory, any guy would think that's a fantastic situation. But let's keep it real. As I mentioned previously, there's only so much Sitch to go around. I decided to deflect the decision-making responsibility away from myself and onto the girls. I approached the hottest chick and said, "Look, obviously I'm The Situation, but I'm not Superman with a rod of steel. As much as I'd love to do all nine of you simultaneously, I think we all know it's not going to happen. So, some have to go while others can stay. Decide amongst yourselves."

The hottest chick huddled with her group of friends then said to me, "Well, we don't like those bitches over there."

For once, female cattiness was playing to my advantage. I tasked her and her friends with eliminating that faction from the room and told them that, when the axe had fallen, to report back to me. That got us down to six, which was a workable number. I was willing to do six.

The six remaining girls split into two groups of three and started arguing in front of me. That's one of those things that dangles right on the edge of being a turn-off or a turn-on. They were all acquainted in some way and were threatening each other that this girl "better not tell her boyfriend what she did tonight," and that girl "better keep her mouth shut to so-and-so." That confrontation transitioned into who was going to start The Situation and who was going to finish him. To my mind, they had finally moved on to a reasonable discussion. I had my preference but, all in the same, I decided to hang back and see how things shook out. While this drama unfolded, I started to yawn. My eyelids were feeling heavy and I couldn't help but think of my early flight and all the hassles of the day's travel that lay ahead. Whatever these chicks were going to decide, they needed to do it fast.

An agreement was reached and I got to work with three of the girls while the other three watched. Out of the corner of my eye, I noticed one of the girls from the on-deck circle retrieving something out of her bag. I've become ultra perceptive of those hijinks—no matter what I'm in the middle of doing. The voice in my head (which sounds just as handsome as my real voice) said, "Dude, you should've collected all their phones and cameras and locked them in the safe." Sure enough, one of the girls was getting her camera to record the festivities. Luckily I wasn't so deep into my situation that I couldn't leap up and whack away her camera (with my *hand*). That nonsense was an immediate deal breaker. I banished her and her two friends from the room for her foolish transgression. They left peacefully, and though I was a little sad to see them go, I was also relieved that I was free to complete my work. Which is exactly what I did.

Life is a battle, bro. It's survival of the fittest. And by fittest, I mean hottest.

SITCH AB FACT: I recently brought three girls back to my hotel room. After a little bit of fun, I realized I was down to two girls. It took me thirty minutes to discover the missing chick was lost in a crevice in my six-pack.

One-Night Stand Checklist
(Multiple Chicks Edition)

- Have a dozen condoms.
- Double-check group to be certain there are no dudes.
- Confiscate all cell phones and cameras, lock in hotel safe. (If no safe, hide them in your abs.)
- Distribute an individual "safe word" to each chick.
- Establish your ground rules (i.e., no pretzels in bed).
- Officiate round of rock, paper, scissors to see who goes first.

Sitch Sez

As The Situation, I need to be aware at all times of the whereabouts of possessions like my cell, wallet, and jewelry. Believe it or not, some girls steal things as a memento of our experience together, as if smooshing isn't enough.

Once, after a sold-out club appearance in Canada, I decided to invite a girl back to my hotel for the night. We were starting to undress when I noticed her rummaging through her bag for her camera. She actually wanted to snap a shot or shoot some video while we were getting naked. I told that head case, "Sorry, baby, but you gotta leave."

Another time I was with this chick I was getting a really weird vibe off of. She always had her cell phone in plain sight, which isn't that unusual, but I sensed that she was positioning it within range of my voice whenever I moved around the room. Plus she was asking me very bold questions like, "Have you ever done this drug before," etc. She was trying to pull it off in a nonchalant way, but I became convinced she was trying to record our conversation. I was reluctant to call her on it because I wasn't positive and I didn't want to suddenly turn into a jerk. But my weird feeling persisted so I finally checked her phone, and sure enough, she was recording. I try to always be polite and give people the benefit of the doubt, but when I caught her red-handed, no matter how hot she was (and she was hot), I kicked her ass out.

It's sad to say, bro, but whenever I hang with chicks in my hotel room (particularly if more than one is involved), I ask them to turn off all electronic devices—or, switch them to Sitch Mode, which means get rid of them. That's why I've started confiscating their phones and cameras and locking them in the room safe. Call it paranoid, but the last thing I want is a video of me doing work showing up on TMZ the next day. Especially if I was having an off night (which, to be honest, is pretty frickin' rare).

The Deadly Clinger

Sometimes you smoosh a chick and decide that you'd like to smoosh that chick again in the future. It's rare, but it happens. Here you must tread with extreme caution, my brothers. You might unwittingly be cultivating a Clinger. Below are the five stages to watch out for:

FIVE STAGES OF CLINGER

1. Sends too many text messages (more than three unsolicited, unresponded-to texts per day).
2. Inappropriate Facebook postings.

3. Knocks on door of unlisted home address—
   unannounced, uninvited, and un-hot.
4. Rolls up to you in the club when you're doing work on
   other targets, thereby becoming Captain Cockblock of
   the Century.
5. Certified Stalker Bitch. At every personal appearance.
   Jealous of your relationship with your mother and
   sister, etc. Pauly D, who dealt with his own stalker
   situation, had to drop this knowledge on his Stage Five
   Clinger: "You're stalking my life. You're stalking my
   whole life on the boardwalk." If you suspect you're
   dealing with a Stage Five situation, I suggest you tie a
   bell around her neck. Tell her it's from Tiffany's.

SITCH AB FACT: Confused after college, my abs backpacked around western Europe, filling dozens of journals with romantic poetry. After six weeks of meditative wandering, they snapped their pencil, decided to get totally ripped, and crush it forever-after down The Shore.

PART III

As Per Life

nine

MANGIA

My mother is like any other good Italian mom. She instilled in me those important values of good food and good fun, surrounded by friends and family. When you look at my astonishing physique you probably think to yourself, *This kid must eat nothing but molten steel.* That's a common misconception. And while I do focus on foods that fuel my body rather than sap it of its energy, I enjoy a wide range of culinary delights. Each day, I rise eager to face whatever new challenges are thrown my way. To remain alert until the wee hours of the morning, when I'm still bumping in the club (or motorboating in the Jacuzzi), I'm picky about the foods I consume and treat my body like the temple it is.

Sitch Sez

I eat six meals a day. Working out as hard, and as often, as I do burns a lot of calories (for example, right now I'm writing this chapter while donkey pressing four hundred pounds). Whether you're cooking chicken cutlets, chicken

Parm, chicken piccata, chicken Marsala, chicken scampi, chicken Francese, chicken cacciatore, or just chicken, the secret ingredient to every meal is love. And also garlic.

My whole approach to cooking is that there's no challenge in the kitchen that intimidates me. I'm willing to take a shot at preparing any recipe. I remember once during the taping of the first season of *Jersey Shore* someone asked if I knew how to cook lobsters. I said, "No. But I'll give it a try." I didn't know what I was doing but I'm not afraid to give *anything* a try. Except doing dudes. I'm just not down for that. Sorry, guys.

If you want to crush it like The Sitch, you can't go skipping your first of the six meals of the day. Hesitation equals flab, so the second you rise, you need to get your wake-up smoothie into you. Pronto.

Building the World's Best Lasagna

In an oven dish, brown 85 percent lean ground beef with minced onion and fresh garlic. Let simmer.

Make your homemade sauce by combining one can tomato paste, two large cans of crushed tomatoes, salt and pepper, basil and garlic, and two tablespoons of sugar.

Add the homemade sauce to the beef, leaving some left over to top off the lasagna.

Beat together ricotta and Parmesan cheese with basil, oregano, and one egg. Then put it all together.

Do NOT cook the lasagna noodles first! Proceed to layer in a deep dish (see diagram). Sprinkle a Parm/mozzarella mix on top and pop it in the oven at 350°F for one hour. Mangia!

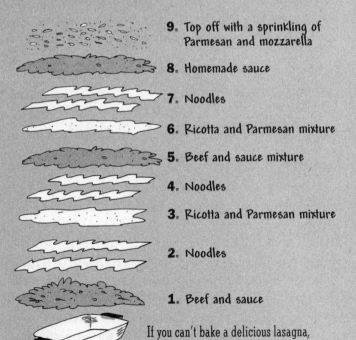

9. Top off with a sprinkling of Parmesan and mozzarella

8. Homemade sauce

7. Noodles

6. Ricotta and Parmesan mixture

5. Beef and sauce mixture

4. Noodles

3. Ricotta and Parmesan mixture

2. Noodles

1. Beef and sauce

If you can't bake a delicious lasagna, get the fuck outta my face.

Eating is a social activity. If you're going to coordinate a feast, you should not be eating it standing at your kitchen counter. Sit down like a human being, surround yourself with good friends and family, and enjoy a little wine and conversation. It's good for the digestion.

If there are any problems or issues amongst your peeps, the family-style dinner is the time to fix them. If Joey got twisted the night before and started creeping on Tommy's chick, let them work it out over pasta fazool. How is anyone going to stay mad when the food is so good?

When it comes time to clear and wash the dishes, the rule is simple: If you cooked the feast, you don't lift a finger to clean up. It's karma, baby (again: not the club, the Eastern philosophy). What you put out in the universe, the universe sends back to you. So, if you cook a meal with love, then that love comes back to you in the form of manual labor. Hey, I'm the man of the house. I can't loosen my belt and take a nap if I'm elbow-deep in Palmolive. That's just physics.

Eating Out
(At a Restaurant, That Is)

A great way to show a lady she's special is to take her to a classy establishment for a fine meal. Good food and a romantic atmosphere is the ideal setting to lay the important groundwork for subsequent smooshing.

I begin every date by being polite and sweet to my lady, which means I open up every door for her, pull out her chair, help her with her order, lift my T-shirt so she can inspect my abs—whatever is going to make her feel more comfortable and at ease with The Sitch. Especially on a first date. One mistake you want to avoid is looking like a clown by showing up at a restaurant having forgotten to make a reservation. The worst way to start a date is with both of you sitting on some bench for forty-five minutes like you're waiting for a Greyhound at Port Authority. Repeat after Sitch: "I will make a reservation." You're going to be a gentleman and a class act all the way on your date by calling ahead to make all the arrangements. You're going to arrive on time and you're going to make sure you're seated at a nice table away from the noise at the bar and that swinging door to the kitchen (unless the waitresses are really hot and you want to check them out as they shuttle back and forth).

It's a smart move to bring a first date to a restaurant you often frequent; a place where you know the staff and you're confident that you'll receive top-notch service. Being on a first-name basis with the staff and being given the red carpet treatment doesn't hurt when it comes to impressing a classy chick. And, yeah, you can't go wrong taking a first date to an Italian restaurant. The food and the atmosphere at a great Italian restaurant are pretty straightforward, allowing you to focus on the time you're spending with each other. Some bros consider dinner a necessary evil as interlude before climbing naked together into the Jacuzzi. (For the record, it is, but you can't let on that it is.)

The last thing you want to do is pick up your date, start driving blindly out on the Parkway, then turn and say, "That place looks good, I guess. Let's eat there." If you roll up to a place out of the blue, having never been there before and having done zero recon, that's the moment your date will know you're a clown. Maybe you've been to the Olive Garden in Toms River, NJ, but does that mean you can trust that the Olive Garden in Eatontown, NJ, will be just as classy? Do you know for a fact that the chicken scampi will be succulent and the breadsticks unlimited at this strange new Olive Garden? No, dude, you don't. Because you didn't do your recon. You can nail the GTL and the GTL Remix, but you can't fake being a class act. Crushing the restaurant scene is no different than crushing your abs: You've got to do the work, bro.

Do I Order for the Lady?

Some guys make a rule of ordering for their dates after they discuss her likes and dislikes. This can be seen by her as macho and/or gentlemanly, but it can also backfire hard-core. The rule for this element of any date is that every situation is a different situation and every chick is a different chick. That's why I say I like my clothes like my women . . . options. But don't make the mistake of presuming that one thing you did in the past that impressed a chick is going to then impress every chick thereafter. That philosophy is not respectful to the hot lady seated across the table from you. Being bold depends a lot on the vibe you're feeling on a particular date. As a general rule, I prefer to remain polite and sweet and defer to her preference by saying things like, "Honey, would you like to have an appetizer or a salad? What sort of things do you enjoy?" Or, "Hey, I've never tried this dish before, would you like to try it together?" Or, "Would you like to eat dessert off my genitals or should I eat it off yours?" Make it about her and not you. Be confident, but keep the lines of communication open because, if you act too boldly, she may already be thinking, "If he's making my decisions for me at this early stage, what trouble does that foretell for our future?" Keep it simple, dawg. Your primary objective is to get the evening's focus out of her head, onto the table, and hopefully later, under your sheets.

Sitch Sez

I maintain a strict diet all week, but allow myself a wide latitude on one special day per week which I call "Cheat Day." So, if I want to have a piece of my mom's cheesecake, or kill a guy, it's all good. Pretty much anything goes on Cheat Day.

Women as Food

I've often heard women referred to as "pieces of meat," which is just crass. The very idea of categorizing a beautiful woman as a food item is absurd. Especially when not properly defined, as I'm about to do now:

Filet Mignon: This hottest of the hot chicks is totally DTF and will yield to a butter knife (like, say, Vinny). Her fat has been completely trimmed, so there's not a ton of flavor, but she melts in your mouth all the same. (A plumper version is known as the Filet wrapped in bacon.)

New York Strip: This should really be renamed the New Jersey Strip, but that's a debate for another time. The key is that this strip won't strip right away. She takes some work. And some extra chewing. But she's definitely worth the effort.

Brisket: This chick is completely unrelenting through the first few hours but gradually becomes pliant and tender when marinated in the proper liquid.

Dry-aged (aka the Cougar Cut): She's been out in the salt air for some time. An expensive taste. But nice depth of flavor.

The bottom line is that they should all be cooked to a crisp on the outside while remaining pink and juicy on the inside.

It's all about caring for your body and making smart choices about how you treat it and what you put inside it. That is, unless you're a chick I'm creeping on at the club. In that case you should keep a very open mind about what you put inside your body. Specifically, me.

ten

YOUR LIFE PARTNER

I tend to rotate through relationships with women at a faster pace than the average creeper. This high turnover rate has helped me fine-tune my various philosophies on life and love. I don't want to waste a girl's time if we both know we're not meant to be together. Eventually, when I find the right girl, I won't need to make any excuses or offer any explanations because everything will feel right and we'll both know it.

Because I'm a famous TV dude, women throw themselves at me. But it's for all the wrong reasons. When it comes to love, I know I need to yank a lot of weeds to get to the flowers. It's hard for me to know these days, since The Situation has become a household name, if a girl is showing feelings toward me because of my fame or because of who I am as a person. In a sense it's as though the roles have reversed. Now I have to be the one to scrutinize the motivations and sincerity of any girl that's creeping on me. I wouldn't say that I put my guard up more—because I rarely do that, if at all—it's just that I'm navigating uncharted territory and learning as I go from my occasional mistakes and my epic successes.

Real-Life Situation

Love can happen in an instant. One afternoon I was shopping in the mall. Through the glass of a shoe store I spotted a beautiful girl with long, dark hair. I did a complete double take. I thought, "Wow! Who is that?" Any time I stop cold like that, there is definitely a primal attraction.

What's interesting is that, in the same split second, she glanced up and noticed me, too. Our eyes locked. Later, I had an opportunity to introduce myself to her. In a one-on-one moment with her friend I said, "Listen, I think your friend is gorgeous."

She said, "No way, my friend just said the exact same thing about you."

And it was on. An instantaneous connection was made and our relationship flourished from that moment forward. We dated for two years.

The Levels of Chick

In my years of playing the game I've come to this conclusion: There are different levels of chick. It's like an inverted pyramid with the wide part at the top—this is your mix of grenades, land mines, and other low-hanging fruit—tapering into the narrowest classification of female that exists: Girlfriend Material, or perhaps even, "The One." Once you get beyond the riff-raff at the club (i.e., grenade launchers, zoo creatures, hypnotic hyenas, trash bags, etc.), girls break down into five categories, from sleeper to keeper. Here is my field guide for the classifications of chick that every creeper should know:

Fifth Class

Oftentimes, a guy might look at a chick and think, "She's hot but not girlfriend hot." Sometimes the reality is that a guy will see a girl and have a primal, caveman reaction to her body. He definitely wants to pound her out but doesn't foresee the relationship progressing any further. For a creeper viewing a chick in this way, it is a purely physical attraction with little to no emotional attachment. This caveman principle operates both ways, of course. Once again, science informs us. A recent peer-reviewed report published by the Creeper Institute of Situationomics states definitively that a woman will choose a man who's physically fit and sexually desirable. A man who exudes confidence and strength to a potential mate over his pastier, doughier, and less Italian-American rival, resulting in the eventual disappearance of that rival's inferior DNA from the gene pool.

Fourth Class

At this level, a guy is attracted to a girl physically, and freely bangs her, but he can't determine if she's cute enough to take her around with him to places where she'll be seen—especially by his bros. As a result, the guy finds himself constantly watching movies on her couch. This strategy soon becomes conspicuous. Before long the girl will ask herself, "Why is this guy not taking me out to dinner? Why is he always making excuses for why we don't go out together? How many more times can we watch *Sopranos* episodes on HBO On Demand?" Truth is, the guy is making excuses to her because he already made up his mind at the jump what classification she falls into: Guidette, Fourth Class.

Third Class

A good-looking girl who's on the wrong side of gorgeous. Not a love-at-first-sight-type girl, but still, someone you're vibing with instantly and want to take out on a real date. Nothing crazy, just a basic date to see what happens. What the guy has decided at the outset is that he doesn't mind being seen with her in public, so he starts simple by taking her to a movie. That's a safe first excursion into the world together because she's only briefly viewed in public (moving swiftly from the vehicle to the door). Then for the rest of the date you're safely hidden inside a dark theater.

Second Class

Then there is the drop-dead gorgeous girl that you definitely want to be seen out with. This is a girl you're going to invite to dinner, giving her the benefit of your full GTL and GTL Remix rituals. This is a girl who makes you want to look and feel your freshest and be on your best behavior. You put real effort into courting this girl because you're willing to see where the relationship leads.

Sitch Sez

Too many chicks mistakenly assume that just because a guy asks them out on a date, she has firmly secured her positioning at the Date Level (Third Class or above). Not necessarily so. To determine her true classification, she must evaluate the actual time she's spending with a guy, and most important, the quality of that time. A beautiful girl who is out to dinner with a guy most certainly believes this to be a normal activity and that all girls are treated in this same fashion. She believes that a guy will spend his hard-earned resources on every girl he's attracted to. She believes this because she's beautiful and blissfully unaware that millions of busted grenades, land mines, and zoo creatures, all around the world, must struggle to earn those date night opportunities. In short, she's spoiled because she's super-hot.

First Class All the Way

Beautiful, smart, classy, and cooks a mean chicken cutlet. Could be "The One." This is no chick, this is a *lady*. She's the girl you take home to meet your mom.

A common mistake guys make is in treating a girl—any girl—like gold. It's the law of diminishing returns, bro. If you always treat a girl like a princess, she's going to get bored. You present no challenge for her. Take it from The Sitch, girls want to work for love. If one person in the relationship is doing all the pushing, and no one is pushing back, that's not a good situation. In life, or in banging.

A Word on Leapfrogging

It is possible, but extremely rare, for a chick to leapfrog levels. To do this, she must exhibit hidden qualities that erroneously placed her at the incorrect level at the jump. Like, say, being double-jointed.

To review:

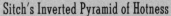

Sitch's Inverted Pyramid of Hotness

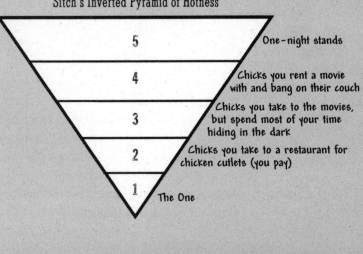

5 One-night stands

4 Chicks you rent a movie with and bang on their couch

3 Chicks you take to the movies, but spend most of your time hiding in the dark

2 Chicks you take to a restaurant for chicken cutlets (you pay)

1 The One

Real-Life Situation

There are two sides to the relationship coin. A girl once creeped on me. What complicated our potential relationship was that it wasn't necessarily love at first sight from my perspective. Don't get me wrong, she was smokin' hot. I just wasn't immediately certain she belonged in my Girlfriend Material classification. First off, she wasn't really my type. She was blond and at the time I was more attracted to dark-haired Italian girls. But I was open to new possibilities and eager to see where our time together might lead.

We were in the same college class together, playing flirtatious games with stolen glances and half-hidden smiles. One day she approached me after class, handed me her number, and told me to call. I was definitely impressed by her assertiveness. Being confident isn't a one-way street and I appreciate a woman who goes after what she wants. I soon realized that this girl was a real beauty—in looks and personality. Before long, she was true Girlfriend Material, headed home with me to meet my parents. We dated for about three years, but eventually, I had to move on to fresh bangs.

eleven

GIVING BACK

After long days and nights of working the GTL lifestyle, crushing it at the club, and smooshing hotties, most creepers would either collapse from exhaustion and severe dehydration, fizzle out like some half-assed firecracker, or simply hole up in their crib for weeks at a stretch to claw back up to their game-day level. But as The Situation, I know I have a responsibility to the greater good. My mission on this planet is to go hard 24/7 until everyone is looking mint, feeling fresh to death, and walking the streets of a Grenade-Free America. That's why I've created the Grenade-Free Foundation. As its founder and president, I'm committed to helping those less fortunate than myself—whether it be feeding the homeless (see Real-Life Situation, next page), or encouraging the visually deficient to hit the gym hard, get some color, and purchase clothing that's properly tailored to their physique. Not unlike Batman (one badass creeper, BTW), while my fellow citizens of the world are engaged in horizontal slumber, I'm out there making this a better planet for us to live on, one situation at a time.

Real-Life Situation

Not long after I landed in Florida for an event, in order to maintain my rigorous nutrition schedule, I made a stop at a gas station convenience mart to purchase a quick protein shake. I'm to a point where my routine is so ingrained that I start to get hungry every two hours, just like an alarm clock going off inside my rock-hard stomach (it makes a sound like a hammer striking an anvil).

I was wearing a rather stylish, flashy jacket, so I was easily recognizable at the gas station and was approached by a few people filming me with their digital cameras. As I posed for some photographs and signed autographs for the group, I noticed an unfortunate gentleman hovering off to the side who looked like he was down on his luck. He came up to me and asked me if I could spare a quarter. A quarter! I was so taken aback by his modest request that I said, "What're you gonna do with a quarter, bro? Y'know what, I think I can spare a little more than that. Are you hungry?"

He said, "Yeah. I am."

"I'd like to buy you a meal. Whaddya feel like eating?"

He looked across the street and said, "Wendy's."

Being as health conscious as I am, I didn't think that was the most nutritious choice he could make, but I wasn't going to argue with him, so I said I would accompany him across the street to Wendy's. But then he noticed that the restaurant section was closed and only the drive-thru was open. He said, "No, that's okay. But can you buy me a dozen eggs here in the mini mart?"

We went inside together and he grabbed a carton of eggs from the cooler.

I said, "You need anything else, dawg?"

"I could use some butter."

He grabbed a pound of butter and I said, "How about chips? You like chips?"

"Yes."

"Grab a selection of chips. In a variety of flavors. Knock yourself out."

He gathered up some bags of chips and I said, "C'mon, that's all you want? Stock up, man. Grab whatever you want."

I'm not saying I'm Mother Teresa or anything. But whatever. This happened.

In my mind I was thinking about how much money I'm offered to show up at a club for a couple hours and this guy doesn't have food to eat. I couldn't imagine a dollar figure that he could ring up at the register of this gas station mini mart that would concern me. He filled his basket with some juice, some macaroni and cheese, canned soups, and some other staples for a very modest grand total of about $60 for three bags of groceries. I was happy to tug the bills out from the bottom of my fat roll. I gave him the change, shook his hand, and wished him well. I told him I hoped things started to turn around for him soon. As I left, I saw him walking through the Wendy's drive-thru.

Education

The best way to contribute to society is by educating yourself. Everywhere I go and talk to young people, I try to drop knowledge. I tell them that they can't drop their own knowledge one day if they choose now to drop their books in the trash can. After high school I attended Brookdale Community College in Lincroft, New Jersey, where I earned my Associate Degree in Business Administration. From there I transferred to Kean University in Union, New Jersey. And I ended my foray into higher education at Monmouth University in West Long Branch, New Jersey, where, admittedly, I'm still a few credits short of my bachelor's degree. But who knows, if things keep going the way they are, I might collect a few honorary doctorates before I finish my bachelor's. Seriously though, I believe that everyone should pursue a high-quality education. And I recommend the college experience as a whole because it's such a huge developmental period for a young person out in the world for probably the first time in his or her life. Plus, there ain't no creeping like college-chick creeping.

Situation Commencement Address

Fellow crushers and crushettes. Congratulations! You have rocked your GTL. You have beat up the beat. You motorboated dozens of worthy Jell-O shot girls, dodged grenades, and smooshed with the creepers who won your hearts at the club. Somewhere along the way, presumably, you have also attended classes. In short, you shredded your college experience. But now, it's time to move on. The working world will present you with

While I may not technically have my four-year degree, I do have my Ph. Pauly-D in Crushonomics from M.I.Creep.

many challenges. For instance, I was employed as a personal fit-
ness trainer and sports underwear model before becoming the
star of the number-one-rated cable television program for view-
ers age eighteen to thirty-four. But of course, I don't need to tell
you that, dear graduates, because you fall squarely into that key
advertising demographic. And while weights, underpants, and
reality television were revealed as my true calling, there are
those of you who may choose a different path. To you I say:
Shoot for the stars, and if you hit the moon, that's still okay.
Even if the moon just happens to be sitting like a drone in front
of a computer in a cubicle inside some soulless office park com-
plex. In the club, as in life, each creeps his own creep, in his own
way. So, if I can leave you with a word of advice, it's this: Keep
doing those sit-ups. I know it's difficult. It's uncomfortable and
you want to quit. But don't. This life is about going hard or
going home, and with ripped abs, pretty much like Rambo, your
future is assured. Thank you.

SITCH AB FACT: Last winter my abs foiled
a plot to blow up the Golden Gate Bridge. And I wasn't
even on the West Coast at the time. In recognition of a
grateful nation, President Obama presented me with the
Presidential Medal of Kickin' Ass and Takin' Names, the
highest award a private citizen can receive for
awesomeness.

On Faith

The gym is my church. When you work out as hard as I do, it requires a tremendous amount of mental preparation and endurance. Working out, if you're doing it right, is pain. The prospect of experiencing that pain can discourage a person from returning to the gym with the frequency necessary to have ripped-up abs. But putting your time in at the gym is guaranteed to make you a physically, mentally, and spiritually stronger person. Finding a spiritual footing in this life is about having a strong body, a confident personality, and a generous spirit. You don't get many shots in this life to make it big, and sometimes you only get one. You're lucky just to get in the league, let alone sit on the bench, let alone play in the game. I don't believe in taking any of my good fortune for granted. In my life, I've been a regular guy and I've been an international superstar. But the moral of my story is that I like the second thing a lot better.

The Creeper's Prayer

God grant me the stamina to satisfy hot chicks,
the courage to deny grenades,
and the wisdom to know the difference.

twelve

ON FAME AND SUCH

Look, everybody loves me: babies, dogs, hot girls, cougars. I just have unbelievable mass appeal. My demographic stretches from grade-school kids to grandparents. I've had pregnant moms approach me (no one yet to say they're carrying a little situation of their own, knock on wood) who hand me a onesie they want me to sign for their newborn. At one of my appearances in St. Louis, Missouri, a guy fainted. That's not a misprint—a *dude* fainted at the sight of The Situation. In Connecticut, a girl was hysterical crying. She was inconsolable to the point I thought she was at a funeral. So I did the only thing I thought would help: I lifted my shirt. But that just made things worse and she was whisked away by ambulance.

So when I'm out there on the road, smooshing chicks and spreading peace and joy, the public has an expectation that they're going to get The Situation. But listen, dawg: What about Mike Sorrentino? What about that kindhearted boy from New Jersey with a tub of protein powder and big dreams? Does he get lost in all this?

And that's why you have to always keep it real. Sometimes The Situation is tired after a long day of being awesome. He just wants to crash in his hotel bed rather than pound out one more really hot fan. But then I think back to Mike Sorrentino, that young go-getter trying to make it in corporate America, hitting the gym, and dreaming of a career as a professional underpants model. Would he turn away a fan? Never.

Germ Warfare

One thing a lot of fans never think about when a famous person is out in public is being aware of good hygiene. Catching a virus or even something as simple as a head cold can put me out of commission for a few days. That can be costly not just to me, but also to pretty much the world economy. When I sneeze, markets crash.

I'm a rookie to all this adulation, so I'm learning as I go. Through trial and error I've started making frequent trips to the restroom to wash my hands, and I carry a container of antibacterial hand sanitizer with me at all times. I make it a rule to never accept any drinks from strangers because I have to be careful who I'm swapping spit with, and sad to say, I need to be wary of what some people might try to slip into my beverage. And before any chick gets in my bed I make her slide into a 200-degree Jacuzzi to sterilize any microbial bacteria that might endanger my health.

Being on TV

If you follow my rules for GTL and beyond, you're eventually going to find yourself on TV talk show The key here is to concentrate on the moment and have a casual conversation with the host, just like you're in your own living room. It doesn't matter if it's Jay, Conan, Ellen, Rachael Ray, George Lopez, Wendy Williams, the cast of *The View*, Jimmy Fallon, or Jimmy Kimmel, or even Ashton Kutcher on his Twitter broadcast, it's just another human being that you're chatting with. It's not that hard if you *don't* think about it. I think the reason so many people connect with me through the camera is because I don't pretend to be anything I'm not. What you see is what you get with The Situation. Who could pretend to be this handsome and charming?

Fashion Tip: On Product and Bling

On television, you need to tailor your wardrobe to the colors and outfits that the camera loves best without sacrificing your signature look. One bonus to your fame will be the ability to spend a little more money on the products and clothes that will aid you in showcasing your personal style and help you look your best. Not only does your improved financial situation allow you to buy the exclusive creams and gels that treat your hair and face right, having more money will reduce your stress levels and your worry lines will magically disappear.

Without going too crazy, you'll also be able to purchase many of the unique and trendy accessories, such as jewelry and watches, that you've long had your eye on but didn't fit your budget. There's no question that a healthy checking account promotes a healthy glow to your skin, a healthy wardrobe, and adds an extra spring in your step. And on the subject of my checking account, my grateful local bank has just completed construction on a private fitness room where I alone am free to do curls and squats with bars that have been thrust into my copious bricks of cash.

Being on TV (cont.)

One convenience for many talk show appearances is that they all basically operate along the same format. Before long you know what to expect from the moment you arrive until you hit the air. Depending on what outfit I'm going to wear appropriate to my appearance, I usually arrive at the studio already dressed and ready to go. There are also times where I arrive straight from the airport with my luggage and need to make a quick change in the dressing room, which barely leaves enough time for The Shirt Before the Shirt.

About a half hour before air I get some touch-ups in the makeup chair, although there's very little that even the pros can do to improve The Situation's skin. After that I'm mic'd up, which means a mobile transmitter is slid into my back pocket, the wire is threaded under my shirt across my rock-hard abs (wrapped in the Kevlar padding that my advance team provides), and a microphone is pinned to my collar. When I'm good to go, the production staff lets me know how much time remains before air and I hang in the green-room (which is never green) watching the program happening in the studio, enjoying the snacks and beverages that have been provided. When I'm led onto the stage I try not to pay much attention to the studio audience. It sounds silly, but the first few times I had to concentrate on just walking over to greet the host without falling—that's how unfamiliar and nerve-racking an experience it can be to the uninitiated. But once in the chair, it's time to settle in and get down to the business of giving America what it craves: more Sitch.

Travel Perks

If you are a traveler, like me, then you know it's tough to maintain a serious diet and fitness routine when you're always on the go. When I'm not filming my show, I'm hitting three or four cities a week, living out of a suitcase, spending long nights in dark clubs and many daylight hours 30,000 feet above the earth. Believe me, it's not easy to stick to the plan when you're on the road, but your life will dial into focus significantly if you remember The Situation's one, golden rule: You must plan your life around the gym.

That might sound crazy, but trust me, it's not. You're probably thinking, "Plan my life around the gym? That's insane! I have a life, Situation!" Well, let me tell you, you're not going to have a long life if you don't take care of yourself. If you don't take care of your body, everything in your life starts to deteriorate.

When you do fly, you want to do it in first class. But a word of caution: When you decide to make the leap forward into first-class seating, be certain that your situation is firmly established. Because once you go first class, you'll never be able to return to coach. Don't cobble together your money for a first-class ticket if you can only afford to do it once. That's faking a situation, not making a situation. Do it like I do it: Make MTV pay for your first-class flights and accommodations. If you're not yet on MTV, go back to the GTL until you are. Don't put the cart before the horse.

Real-Life Situation

Recently I arrived very late for my flight departing from the Houston airport. To my dismay, there was a massive amount of people waiting in lines that stretched for hours at both the check-in counters and the security gate. I knew with one look that there was no chance I was going to make my flight. I started walking through the terminal toward where I needed to be. I usually travel incognito, wearing a hat and sunglasses so I don't draw attention to myself (even though my hat and sunglasses are so fresh, they usually draw their own attention). The danger is, if people see The Situation, a whole airport might shut down. But on this morning in Houston I was not doing anything to conceal my identity. I was hopelessly late for my flight with thirty minutes before my plane took off. I hadn't printed my ticket or checked my bag, let alone considered the long wait through security, so I had accepted my fate. I was not getting on that airplane. As a Hail Mary, I approached one of the female airline representatives and asked her if she knew if my plane was running on schedule to JFK. As soon as she saw my face and heard my voice she lit up and said, in that sweet Texas drawl, "Oh my God! The Situation! It's you, isn't it?"

"It's me."

"Honey, you have got to take a picture with me."

"Anything for you guys. Hey, listen . . . I'm ridiculously late for my flight. Is there anyway you can check me in real quick?"

"Honey, for you, I'll do anything. Follow me, Situation."

She went directly to one of the other airline representatives behind the check-in counter and huddled up with her while all the weary faces in the hour-long line trained their eyes on me. Then, all the women behind the counter stopped checking in passengers and came over to me for a round of photographs and autographs as they checked me in for my flight. From there, they radioed ahead to security and escorted me to the security gate, where I was deposited at the head of the line and immediately ushered through and rushed to my gate. I barely uttered a word as I was whisked from one station to the next. I was blown away that I could go from resigning myself to missing my flight to being raced onto my plane in a matter of minutes.

So, as far as any tricks I might recommend for breezing through security, the best thing I can suggest is that you become a famous person like The Situation. Other than that, you're on your own.

The Fame Bang:
Mile-High Edition

You may ask yourself: How will I know when I have achieved my own situation? I suggest the realization will become apparent the first time a member of the opposite sex is drawn to you purely by their perception of your fame. I had a very memorable experience the very first time I was noticed by a stranger as a television personality. It occurred on the day that *Jersey Shore* was set to premiere on MTV. The teasers and articles had been running nonstop leading up to the airing of the first episode and controversy was swirling before the series had even hit the airwaves. Audiences had already received their first taste of The Situation because I had enjoyed some media exposure as one of the main faces of the show, defending its content and telling everyone to relax—it was just a group of friends out to have a great time together. The day of the premiere, I was waiting for an hour layover in the airport terminal in Charlotte, North Carolina, for my connecting flight to Los Angeles. Seated across from me was a beautiful girl, taking on her cell, who unmistakably kept looking over and smiling at me.

We boarded the plane, and as it turned out, her seat was one row up and diagonal from mine. This is when my wheels started turning. I figured we were hunkered down for a long flight across the country and I wanted to get to the bottom of the vibe I was feeling from this girl. Before I could make a move, she turned to me and said, "Are you Mike 'The Situation' from that Jersey show that's coming out?"

"You know it, girl."

"I thought it was you," she smiled. "It premieres tonight, right?"

"Yes it does."

Being the spur-of-the-moment person that I am, willing to try anything once (see exception on page 94), I was suddenly determined to make the most of this very promising situation. I started thinking this might be my best chance to gain membership into the Mile-High Club. It was something I'd never remotely had the opportunity to do before and I thought this might be my best—or perhaps, my only—chance to pull it off. I made eye contact with her, then looked over my shoulder toward the restroom indicating that we should try to make our way back there together at our first opportunity. To her credit, she smirked and nodded her head, taking my meaning exactly as we forged a wordless confederacy.

In all honesty, the only thought running through my mind was "no fucking way." It's one thing to imagine those kinds of scenarios but quite another when you find yourself in one and start to game plan the logistics of pulling it off. From that moment of silent acknowledgment forward, I watched the rear bathroom like a barn owl with my head turned practically 180 degrees. Just my luck, I

was on a flight where everybody and their grandmother had blad-
der control issues. I had this chick ready to go for over an hour of
flying time and the clowns on my flight were lined up in the rear like
they were waiting for the one Porta-Potty at Woodstock. I was getting pretty frustrated and impatient. And my neck hurt. Finally, the
compartment was unoccupied for an extended period and I was
confident that this was our one shot. I made a show of getting up
and she got the message. I strolled to the back of the plane with her
a few steps behind and, just as I entered the restroom, some fucking
tool stood up and boxed out the chick as she tried to enter in behind
me. This fuck-nut wasn't even doing anything. He stood to blow his
nose and stretch his legs. Meanwhile, I left the door ajar waiting for
the chick, who was unable to get past the guy positioned as a human
cock block between her and the restroom. Then, he noticed me
leaving the door open while I'm standing in the bathroom. He
started gawking at me like *I* was the idiot.

I responded with a facial expression that communicated, "Dude,
are you serious? Why are you preventing the chick standing next to
you from making her way into the bathroom? Open your eyes and
get the fuck back in your seat, asshole!" (Remember that I'm from
Jersey, and can therefore easily convey multilayered fuck-you senti-
ments like this by merely raising an eyebrow.) As it dawned on him
what was happening, he smiled at me and sat back down. The girl
made her way into the restroom and we did our best to accomplish
a very awkward and challenging task. This is another instance
where being organized and prepared pays off. I always travel with
my little black bag in my carry-on that contains certain essentials,
such as condoms, because I never know what sort of curveball life
will throw me. Earning my membership into this exclusive club that
meets only in the clouds was an extremely difficult process that
should not be underestimated. I say it's worth it for the experience
and the novelty aspect, but don't expect it to be one of your most
memorable sexual encounters. It's more about the story and doing

something few people have had the balls to pull off. And we're lucky we didn't hit any turbulence, or my balls literally would have been pulled off.

Some haters say that I'm Machiavellian in the way I insinuate my infectious catch phrases into conversations. They're convinced I come up with all my best lines ahead of time. Allow me to dispel this falsehood. First off, I don't mack any vellians—whatever those are. I only mack chicks, either between sets at the gym or when I'm creeping at the club. And further, everything I say comes straight off the top of my well-tanned head. Period. Emoticon.

As Per Haters

Whenever you attempt to do something extraordinary in your life, whenever you put yourself out there in an attempt to succeed and in turn risk falling flat on your face, there are going to be people on the sidelines second-guessing you and making fun of you as a mechanism to disguise their own fear and envy for the life they're watching you achieve. Those people are called haters.

Attention, haters: It's been a lot longer than fifteen minutes.

A hater is weak, jealous, insecure, and preoccupied in an unhealthy way with tearing down the accomplishments of others. What a hater should really be worried about is himself. Rest assured that when you get your own situation, you will be vilified by the haters. That's because they want what you have, whether it be looks, money, fame, your girl, your abs, your T-shirt wardrobe, or what have you. In fact, being positive and confident is like kryptonite to haters. But the good news is: Hater juice is best served cold.

I think the best way to think about haters is this: If somebody's talking about you, that means you're doing something right. If they're jealous of what you have and are projecting their venom and their miserable attitude in your direction, that must mean you're pretty important. For some reason they can't properly articulate, you're on their mind. And even though a hater would never admit it, in some way they are holding your life up as a standard for their own that they have not yet attained. People who are comfortable with their own personality and circumstances don't have the desire to hate on others. If somebody is hating on you, I think you should be flattered. It means you're out there kicking it hard-core.

I don't ever want to forget about the haters. The haters have worked tirelessly, in a thousand different ways, to make *Jersey Shore*, and myself, worldwide sensations. So I would be remiss if I didn't send a great big shout-out to all the haters. Thanks for all your efforts; they have been wildly successful. Keep it up, dawgs!

Real-Life Situation: Trouble at The Cheesecake Factory: A Cautionary Tale

Like a typical Jersey guy, I hit up my local mall when I need to go shopping. I like to support the merchants in my community and I'm always happy to stop and take pictures, give autographs, or chat with fans who approach me. And if someone needs to massage my abs, I try to work it into my busy schedule.

One day at the mall, my boys and I decided to pop into The Cheesecake Factory for a quick bite. There was a mob scene of patrons waiting inside the doors so I had my good friend, The Unit, go inside to check on the availability of a table. By the way, The Unit, who was my college roommate, is almost always at my side. He has got mad game all his own and there's no doubt that America will be seeing much more of him very shortly. So, The Unit approached the hostess and said, "Look, I've got The Situation with me. Do you have any tables?"

She seemed physically pained by the predicament The Unit was putting her in. She said, "Y'know, it's a ninety-minute wait. He's a very recognizable face. If we bring him in here ahead of all these people who have been waiting for so long, it would no doubt cause a lot of animosity and might be viewed in a very negative light for both the restaurant and for The Situation. That being said, we'll do the best we can."

"No problem," said The Unit. "We don't want to make trouble."

As The Unit turned to head back outside, the hostess said, "Actually, there's a seat at the bar and you're welcome to sit there or gather around that area and order lunch if you're comfortable with that."

With that reconnaissance, The Unit stepped outside and informed The Situation of the situation inside The Cheese-cake Factory. We decided to lunch at the bar. As we entered, I could see and hear all the people waiting inside the doors turning and murmuring to each other, "There he is. The Situation." We took a seat at a high table by the bar in the area the hostess directed us to and settled in with our menus. The waiter took our drink orders. So far, so good.

Suddenly, the manager materialized and said, "Y'know, guys, technically this table is part of the restaurant area and not the bar. A lot of people just watched you enter and take this table ahead of them after they've been waiting for quite a long while. Obviously they recognize you as a world-famous television personality with ripped-up abs and a tight fade [I'm paraphrasing] and some of them are very angry. They feel that we've given you preferential treatment and that's not our policy here at The Cheesecake Factory."

I said, "Honestly, I had no idea this table was designated one way or the other. I just followed The Unit, who got his information from your girl at the door. I'm not trying to upset anybody or spoil their lunch experience. We sat down where we were directed to sit down and your waiter took our drink order like everything was fine. If you want us to move, we'll move. It's not a big deal."

"Unfortunately, at this stage it's not going to be that simple," said the manager. "One of our angry patrons has already called the police."

"The police? What would be the charge, exactly, once they arrive? Unlawful sitting? To tell you the truth, I'm looking forward to their arrival because I'm fascinated by what they're going to say to The Situation and The Unit about this particular situation."

"I apologize for the confusion," said the manager. "May we accommodate you with a table at the back of the restaurant? With or without law enforcement on their way, there's already quite a scene developing with people blocking the entrance to stare or take photographs and video."

So the manager moved me, The Unit, and the rest of our

group to a secluded table in the back of the restaurant. Before long, the police arrived and paid us a visit during our appetizers. They shook our hands and we took some pictures together. No reports were filed.

Leaving the restaurant, we realized I was running late for my next event. We hustled to the car and my buddy, who was driving, tore out of the parking lot way too fast. That prompted another police officer to pull us over. Two run-ins with the police in one afternoon! Now that's a situation.

The police officer said, "Is there a reason why you're exiting this parking lot at such a high rate of speed?"

"I'm sorry, officer," said The Unit. "We're running late for an event tonight with the mayor of New York City and we've got The Situation in the car."

"You've got The Situation in the car?" The officer leaned in to confirm.

"Hello, Situation."

"Hello, officer."

We shook hands. And, I can't be certain, but I swear to this day that I saw a tear streak just below the rim of his mirrored sunglasses. He quickly turned away.

"Okay, you boys are free to go. Creep well tonight, Situation. Do it for New Jersey."

FINAL THOUGHTS

Dear readers, thank you for spending some time with The Sitch. In this unabridged and definitive guide to the GTL lifestyle, I'm pretty sure I have emptied out the entire contents of my brain. Wait, let me double-check . . .

Yes, I have.

And I did it for you. You are the reason The Sitch keeps kicking it hard-core, 24/7. Every morning when I wake up, I go straight to work to make this a grenade-free world for the freshest of the fresh. Right to work, that is, after I kick out whatever chicks are still lingering from the night before. And after I have my protein shake and hit the gym, of course. And get some color, if needed. Quick stop at the barbershop for a touch-up on my tight fade. Thread the eyebrows. Then it's across town to pick up my dry cleaning—but you get the general idea.

You are the wind beneath my abs.

As a special gift, I leave you with this exclusive pattern to sew your own Sitch ab-pillow. Something to gently fondle while you watch me Thursday nights at 10 p.m. on MTV, or just to lay your head upon at night as you dream your Jersey dreams.

The first step is arguably the most difficult: Select a fabric that closely mimics my radiant skin tone. (Tip: Bring home swatches from the store and hold them beside the television whenever I'm on screen. For best results, use HD technology.)

Cut the fabric as shown in a rounded fashion, allowing a half-inch seam around the circumference.

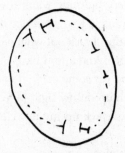

Lay one pseudo-ab atop the other. Pin them together, leaving space for an opening.

Sew around the ab-pillow, leaving that half-inch seam allowance and stopping short of the opening. Turn the pillow right side out and iron it flat.

Visit your local quarry and ask the foreman to fill your pillow with either dense, hard-packed gravel, or a slab of granite cut to size with a wet saw. (Note: Granite is smooth and will best simulate the feel of my actual abdominals, but any rock that registers 7 or more on the Mohs' scale of mineral hardness will do.)

Sew closed the opening with tiny whipstitches. Voila! Enjoy your official Sitch ab-pillow.

Feel free to embroider your new ab-pillow with any of your favorite Sitch quotes. Such as, "Don't push it too far with me or I'll throw you in the trunk." Or, "This situation is gonna be indescribable. You can't even describe the situation that you're about to get into this situation." Or, "Everybody loves The Situation. And if you don't love The Situation, I'm going to make you love The Situation."